THE WEALTH DIARY

Your Personal Financial Record

Foreword by

Shri Nitin Gadkari,
Hon'ble Minister of Road Transport and Highways,
Government of India

DR. NAVIN MUKESH PUNJABI

notionpress.com

INDIA • SINGAPORE • MALAYSIA

द
वेल्थ
डाइरी

तव्हां जो शख़्सी माली दस्तावेज़ु

डॉ. नवीन मुकेश पंजाबी

دَ

ويلٿ

ڊائري

توهان جو شخصي مالي دستاويز

ڊاڪٽر نوين مڪيش پنجابي

ISBN 979-8-89133-856-2

Disclaimer

The information, views, and opinions expressed in this book are those of the author, Dr. Navin M. Punjabi, and do not necessarily reflect or represent the views of any organisations with which he may be affiliated, employed, associated, or to which he may be invited.

While every effort has been made to ensure the accuracy and completeness of the information contained in this Blue Book, it is provided 'as is,' - without warranty of any kind, either express or implied. Dr. Navin M. Punjabi shall not be liable for any errors, omissions, or inaccuracies in the information or for any reliance on or use of this information by any person or entity.

Any references to financial schemes, investments, or tax treatments are provided for informational purposes only and should not be construed as advice or recommendations. Readers are encouraged to consult appropriate professionals, including financial advisers, tax consultants, and legal attorneys, to understand the specific details and risks associated with any referenced schemes or investments, or your own action or non-action.

This Wealth Diary may contain proprietary and/or confidential material belonging to the user/reader, including user IDs, passwords, and other highly personal details. The user/reader understands the importance of keeping this information confidential and acknowledges that keeping the book secure and confidential is solely his responsibility. Any breach of confidentiality could result in severe legal consequences.

By accessing or using this Wealth Diary, the reader acknowledges and agrees to these terms and conditions and indemnifies Dr. Navin M. Punjabi from any liability, claims, or damages arising out of or related to the unauthorised use, interpretation, or dissemination of the information contained herein.

Dedication

This book is dedicated with love to the memory of my father, the late Shri Mukesh Hariram Punjabi. He was an esteemed lecturer in Commerce at Smt. Maniben M.P. Shah Women's College and a respected member of the District Consumer Redressal Forum. As a Special Executive Officer (SEO) for the Government of Maharashtra, he played a significant role.

His profound passion for education, consumer protection, unwavering dedication to his students, and enduring wisdom continue to inspire us. His spirit resonates within the pages of this book, guiding us toward a deeper knowledge and understanding.

Fittingly, this book is complete from my side and sent for editorial reviews in the month of his birthday, a month that also sees India celebrating World Investor Week by IOSCO. This synchronicity stands as a tribute to his significant contributions as an educator and a fervent stakeholder in India's Consumer Protection Movement.

May his memory serve as a radiant beacon and a pillar of strength to all who had the honour of learning from him.

Contents

नितीन गडकरी
NITIN GADKARI

सत्यमेव जयते

मंत्री
सड़क परिवहन एवं राजमार्ग
भारत सरकार
Minister
Road Transport and Highways
Government of India

D. O. No. 2215
DATE 04 FEB 2024

FOREWORD

In the ever-evolving landscape of personal finance, where economic uncertainties and financial complexities often remain dominant, Dr. Navin Mukesh Punjabi's book 'The Wealth Diary' emerges as a beacon of knowledge and enlightenment. I congratulate Dr. Navin for this groundbreaking feat.

This endeavour is not just a compilation of financial advice; rather, it is a transformative journey that aims to enlighten, empower, and equip citizens with the indispensable tools to make informed financial decisions.

Dr. Punjabi's deep-rooted belief in the collective responsibility of all stakeholders to promote financial literacy forms the cornerstone of this invaluable guide. In a world where the understanding of financial matters can be both elusive and overwhelming, "The Wealth Diary" serves as a guiding light, unravelling the intricacies of wealth management and fostering a culture of financial well-being. This book offers the readers a strategic approach as to how to maintain a comprehensive record of their wealth. Dr. Punjabi's insights on the creation and maintenance of this financial blueprints shed light on how this simple yet powerful tool can revolutionize financial planning and decision-making.

Financial wellness, a term often bandied about, is given profound meaning and practical application in "The Wealth Diary."Dr. Punjabi dissects the elements of financial well-being, emphasizing the holistic nature of wealth that extends beyond mere monetary considerations. Through practical advice and actionable strategies, he guides readers toward achieving a state of financial wellness that encompasses emotional, physical, and mental aspects.

A topic often relegated to the shadows, the dormant wealth of unclaimed deposits and dividends is brought into sharp focus in this book. Dr. Punjabi's exploration of this often overlooked aspect serves as a wake-up call, urging readers to be vigilant about their financial affairs.

In a nation as diverse and dynamic as India, where the tints of financial landscape vary from bustling urban centres to remote rural villages, Dr. Punjabi makes a compelling case for universal financial literacy. His impassioned call for every Indian citizen to possess the knowledge to manage, grow, and cherish their wealth responsibly resonates as a clarion call for a more financially inclusive society.

This book is not a dry manual on financial management; it is a compelling and relatable guide that speaks directly to the reader, imparting wisdom and demystifying the world of finance.Dr. Navin Mukesh Punjabi's dedication to enlightening individuals about the power of informed financial decisions, his advocacy for financial literacy, and his insights into the nuances of wealth management make this book a timeless and invaluable resource. I commend Dr. Punjabi for his commitment to fostering a society where financial well-being is not a privilege but a fundamental right for all.

Yours

(Nitin Gadkari)

Room No. 501, Transport Bhawan, 1, Sansad Marg, New Delhi – 110 001, Tel.: (RTH) 011-23710121, 23711252 (O), 23719023 (F), E-mail: nitin.gadkari@nic.in; website-www.morth.nic.in
Camp Office Nagpur : Plot No. 25, Opp. Orange City Hospital, Beside Jupiter School, Khamla Chowk, Nagpur-440015(MS)
Tel.: 0712-2239918/20/22/23/24 Email : office@nitingadkari.net

D. M. HARISH & CO.

ADVOCATES

305-309, "NEELKANTH", 98, MARINE DRIVE, MUMBAI 400 002.
Area Code - International : 00-91-22 National : 022
Telephones : 4334 2000, 2281 7272, 2281 0517
Fax : 2281 3785
E-mail : dmhco@dmharish.com
Website : www.dmharish.com

ADVOCATES :

Mr. ANIL HARISH
Mrs. SHOBHA JAGTIANI
Mr. ADHIRAJ HARISH
Mr. HARI RAHEJA
Mr. BHUPENDRA KENIA
Mrs. YASMIN CARNAC
Mr. PRAKASH JOTWANI
Ms. MRUGAKSHI JOSHI
Mr. MANOJ INDULKAR
Ms. DIVYA ALEXANDER
Mr. PRIYANSHU KHATRI
Ms. ANJALI JHAWAR
Ms. SNEHA AGICHA

CHARTERED ACCOUNTANT :

Mr. NISHIL JAIN

18th October, 2023

As India commemorates its 75th year of Independence, it is imperative for its citizens to introspect on their personal journeys towards financial independence. "The Wealth Diary" by Dr. Navin M. Punjabi stands out as a crucial guide in this endeavour. This isn't just a manual on personal finance management, but an effort to institutionalize the process of recording one's wealth and ensuring the meaningful handover of one's legacy.

Dr. Punjabi's book doesn't merely inform—it elucidates and enlightens. It instils in readers a disciplined approach to financial matters that can shape all aspects of life. The personal anecdotes incorporated serve to humanize the complexities of finance, bridging the gap between theoretical knowledge and its real-world application.

For our younger generation, this book is an essential read, providing them with the tools they need to navigate their financial futures. For the seasoned, it offers invaluable insights to refine and optimize their financial strategies. I wholeheartedly endorse "The Wealth Diary" as a beacon of financial knowledge and a cornerstone for anyone aspiring to chart a sound financial course.

Anil Harish

Anil Harish,
Partner, D M Harish & Company
President, H(S)NC Board

Preface

In the constantly evolving tapestry of life, our financial endeavours, dreams, and legacies are the threads that bind us together, generation after generation. Every individual's financial journey is intricate and unique, deserving of documentation, understanding, and celebration. This journey of mine gave birth to the Wealth Diary, which I call the 'Blue Book.'

In my years of traversing the financial realm, I have come to realise that most of us are not prepared for the myriad financial uncertainties that life might throw our way. The essence of preparation isn't merely in accumulating wealth but in maintaining a meticulous record of it, understanding our assets and liabilities, and ensuring that our loved ones are never in the dark about our financial concerns and decisions.

The Blue Book is not just another financial guidebook. It's a reflection of my experiences, insights, and the stories of countless individuals who, in their distinctive ways, have emphasised the need for a comprehensive financial record. Within its pages, you'll discover the significance of safeguarding your important documents, ensuring they're easily accessible when most needed, and the art of weaving technology into your financial narrative.

Section I delves into the "why" – the compelling reasons behind the creation of such a Diary. Through seven personal anecdotes and reflections in 11 chapters, I aim to impress upon you the importance of maintaining a Wealth Diary. Section II is the practical heart of the book, focusing on the "how" – It offers you a step-by-step guide on documenting your financial journey, leveraging technology, and using innovative techniques like QR codes to convey fundamental messages to your loved ones.

The need for maintaining a 'Wealth Diary' was reiterated by the Honourable Finance Minister of India, Smt. Nirmala Sitharaman, at the Global Fintech Fest 2023, cited that, according to a report, the banking sector alone has more than ₹35,000 crores in unclaimed deposits. Astonishingly, the overall quantum of such unclaimed funds is believed to be in excess of ₹1 lakh crores. The Reserve Bank, on August 17, 2023, launched a centralised web portal UDGAM (Unclaimed Deposits - Gateway to Access Information) to help people search for and claim unclaimed deposits. The finance minister has urged the banking and securities market institutions to ensure all accounts have nominations to address the concerns over rising unclaimed deposits and investments after the death of individuals.

This is where the Blue Book becomes pivotal. For a responsible financial ecosystem to truly thrive, each individual needs to be equipped with the right tools and knowledge. The Blue Book aims to serve as a repository of an individual's financial, personal, and legal information. It can help prevent scenarios where substantial sums of money are left unclaimed due to a lack of proper record-keeping or miscommunication.

In the pursuit of broadening financial literacy and empowering individuals, this book has been crafted not only as a standalone guide but also as a potential inclusion in the financial education resources of regulators, Market Infrastructure Institutions (MIIs), Asset Management Companies (AMCs), and other financial institutions dedicated to Financial Literacy and Investor Awareness Programmes.

But why 'The Blue Book'? Blue, for many, symbolises trust, loyalty, wisdom, confidence, and stability. These are the very tenets upon which our financial aspirations should be built. This Book endeavours to be your trustworthy companion, guiding you toward achieving and preserving your wealth.

In these pages, I invite you to participate in a transformative journey, urging you to institutionalise the process of recording your wealth. Here, you will find more than just techniques and strategies; you will also find a philosophy that champions the cause of financial literacy and wellness.

I hope the Blue Book becomes a cherished tool for you and the generations that follow, illuminating the path of financial prudence and legacy-building.

To wealth, wisdom, and a secure future,

With warm regards,

Dr. Navin M. Punjabi
Author – The Wealth Diary

ज्ञानं न लुण्ठितं न च राज्ञा हर्तुं शक्यते।न भ्रातृषु विभक्तुं शक्यते, न च भारं भवति। वर्धते,यदि नियमितरूपेण प्रयोगः भवति। ज्ञानं महत्तमं विधं धनम्।

Knowledge cannot be robbed, nor can it be taken away by a king. it cannot be divided among brothers, nor does it burden one. It increases,if used regularly. Knowledge is the greatest kind of wealth.

Follow me on

If you wish to request for Soft Copy of Section II of the Wealth Diary kindly scan the QR code below

Endorsements

I had recruited Navin from a leading B School. I thought he was destined to be a Wealth Manager but went on to become a professor. However, his interest in Personal Finance only grew. His **Blue Book** is a testimony of this. This book looks at human emotions and experiences related to financial security. It is an easy book to read and relate to, as the book has been written for the common man.

– Gop Kumar, M.D. & CEO, Axis Mutual Fund.

Financial literacy is the bedrock upon which nations can build a prosperous and stable economic future. "The Wealth Diary: Your Personal Financial Record," authored by Dr. Navin M. Punjabi, is not merely a book but a clarion call for financial empowerment. I see it as a ready reckoner for organising your finance portfolio, contextualised in the personal anecdotes he narrates. The templates provided for recording one's wealth are inclusive and exhaustive, a good effort is made to institutionalise the process of recording one's finances.

To anyone yearning to understand the world of finance and take control of their financial destiny, I wholeheartedly recommend this book. Let it be the compass that steers you toward financial enlightenment and freedom.

– Prof. Rajan Welukar, Vice-Chancellor, Atlas SkillTech University
Former Vice-Chancellor, University of Mumbai

"In 'The Wealth Diary: Your Personal Financial Record' which Dr. Punjabi refers to it as his Blue Book, readers are not just presented with another book on finance, but a powerful tool for genuine financial autonomy. As we rally around the vision of an 'Atmanirbhar Bharat', Dr. Punjabi's meticulous templates and insightful guidelines empower the 'Atmanirbhar Niveshak' – the self-reliant investor. This book enables every individual to grasp their financial future firmly, echoing the broader vision of our nation. It's more than just a read; it's a step towards true financial self-reliance.

– Shri Nehal Vora, MD and CEO, CDSL.

Dr. Navin Punjabi's 'The Wealth Diary' helps readers discover why and how to record their financial history such that it provides an unambiguous account even without the individual's intervention.

Financial record-keeping is an often-ignored aspect of financial education. While people endeavour to maximise their wealth, they neglect to diligently record their financial decisions, etc. It results in the individual and their loved ones staying unaware about their financial assets. INR 35,000 crore lying as unclaimed deposits in our banks testifies to the malaise.

'The Wealth Diary' offers readers a step-by-step guide on documenting their financial journey, leveraging technology, and using innovative techniques like QR codes to convey indispensable messages to their loved ones. Dr. Punjabi, in his simple yet lucid style, has provided tools and techniques to create a comprehensive record of financial assets that helps unlock the true benefits of these assets at the right time.

I recommend 'The Wealth Diary' for creating a fulfilling financial legacy.

– Ms. Radhika Gupta, MD & CEO of Edelweiss Mutual Fund

You don't realize the importance of things till it hits you! Navin has put things out there so candidly and in simple language through personal experiences. Whilst reading I am guilty of neglecting a few things, am sure, many would come to a similar realization. Thanks, Navin, for coming out with such a simple yet often neglected part of our lives. A must read and a must do for all!

– Kaiyomurz Daver, Head – Marketing, Bandhan AMC

Over the years, many authors have released financial guidebooks. However, Dr. Navin Punjabi's book "The Wealth Diaries: Your Personal Financial Record", which he fondly also calls the "Blue Book" is unique in that- he is sharing his own very personal real stories, experiences, and learnings that he has gained over the years from his family, his stints with Kotak Securities, DBS bank and research over the years while working as Vice Principal of - H.R. College Mumbai.

I am very sure, this book will help many people to build skills, habits, and to manage their assets and their wealth. This book is innovative, clear and able to open pathways for the common person towards financial literacy, use of technology for investment, creating awareness about financial uncertainties, managing wealth and particularly recording it so that the eventual purpose of wealth – i.e. Charity and Succession can be achieved without complications.

I wish Dr. Navin Punjabi the very best as he moves forward in creating financial awareness for the common man in a robust and practical manner.

– Shri Lal Chellaram

Chairman - Chellaram Foundation & Trustee – HSNC Board

Dr. Navin Punjabi's book "The Wealth Diary" is a must read which should be kept in all financial and educational institutions, government organisations as well as every household that cares about the wellbeing of their loved ones. This book is nothing short of a financial roadmap guiding you through every step of the wealth-building and documentation journey. I was amazed by the practicality of the advice given in "The Wealth Diary". It does not just talk about vague concepts. It provides actionable strategies that anyone can follow. Whether you are a beginner, someone with financial knowledge or highly technology oriented, you will find valuable insights in this book. Weaving his personal experiences and "Black Swan" moments as a trigger to write this book, Dr. Navin gives compelling reasons for everyone to maintain a meticulous record of their financial, personal and legal information.

In a world where financial literacy and financial freedom is more crucial than ever, not only for the individual but for the entire nation, "The Wealth Diary" is a beacon of knowledge and a comprehensive financial guidebook at your fingertips. I highly recommend it to all those looking at not only taking control of their financial future, but also to leave a legacy behind.

– Maya Shahani Chairperson, Shahani Group & Trustee, HSNC Board

Dr. Navin M Punjabi's "The Wealth Diary - Your Personal Financial Record" is an insightful exploration of the complex relationship between life, family, and financial planning. This book is more than just a guide to managing one's finances; it's a journey through Dr. Navin's own life experiences, which have shaped his perspective on wealth and legacy.

Dr. Navin's narrative is touching and relatable, making it easy for readers to connect with his story.

Throughout the book, Dr. Navin emphasizes the importance of maintaining a meticulous financial record, something he calls the "Blue Book." This concept of 'blue book 'is not just a practical guide but a philosophy that champions financial literacy and wellness. It's about securing not just your wealth but your legacy for future generations.

One of the most important takeaways from the book is the idea that wealth is like a family name, an eternal legacy that deserves planning and protection. Dr. Navin's storytelling makes this often-intimidating topic approachable and relatable. Whether you're a financial novice or an experienced investor, this book offers valuable lessons and insights for individuals and families on their financial journey.

I wish Dr. Navin M Punjabi all the best and look forward to more gems of knowledge that benefit the masses.

– Dr. Hemlata K. Bagla

Vice-Chancellor, H(S)NC University, Mumbai

Family financial management is not taught in schools, as a result non-existent financial management is the leading cause of divorces and causes many unnecessary problems in life. I remember living next to a professor's family, who when they got paid fortnightly would go the mall and splurge on non-essentials.

However, two weeks later their children were at our door begging for food, as the family had run out of cash. Navin has produced a very readable guide on how to handle the family finances for everyday life as well as for emergencies. I recommend this book for any family, whatever their circumstances.

– **Dr. Douglas Moodie**, Professor of Management,
Michael A. Leven School of Management, Entrepreneurship and
Hospitality, Kennsaw State University, Georgia, Atlanta, USA

True financial resilience isn't just measured by the amount of wealth one possesses but by the skill with which one manages it. It's about navigating the unpredictable tides of life with a well-chartered map, where not only our assets and liabilities are clearly outlined, but which provides us with a sense of security that we are guarded against the uncertainties of life in the time of crisis. More than being just a personal understanding, it's about ensuring that our near and dear ones are also aware of the same and are not left in the dark, uncertain about our financial path. Wealth grows and diminishes, but a proper financial record and an informed circle stands as an unwavering pillar against life's uncertainties.

In this regard, I am happy to know that a book 'The Wealth Dairy - Your Personal Financial Record' is being brought out by Dr. Navin M Punjabi, which touches this important topic. The author has encapsulated his personal experiences in the book, which would be helpful for the readers not only to understand the intricacies and the importance of financial literacy but also to imbibe the best practices in their daily life to manage their finances more efficiently.

Wishing the readers an insightful experience.

Best regards,

– CA. Aniket Talati, FCA

Acknowledgements

First and foremost, my heartfelt thanks go to my beloved better half, Diya, whose constant support and understanding have been the bedrock upon which this book has been built. Next, to my daughter, Krisha, whose youthful curiosity and enthusiasm continually inspire me to see the world in new ways.

I extend my gratitude to my mother, Nisha, whose unconditional love and wisdom have always guided me. My thanks also to my brother, Manish, his wife, Yahvi, and my nephew and niece, Tej and Sarhana. Their constant support and encouragement have been invaluable throughout this journey.

I extend the same gratitude to Mr. Viraj Singal, my former student, who is the Head of Investor Education and Awareness Initiatives at Krisha Foundation, for his expert critique, which has significantly improved the quality of this book.

My deepest appreciation is extended to Mr. B. Gopkumar, now the CEO of Axis Mutual Fund. As my first corporate mentor, he recruited me at Kotak Securities and groomed me to understand the fundamentals of financial planning and corporate work etiquette; these lessons have profoundly shaped my understanding and approach to this field.

I am eternally grateful to Mr. K. Ramkumar, founder of Leadership Centre, whose immense support during challenging times ensured my family's well-being and provided the necessary grounding for this book's creation.

I owe a great debt of gratitude to Prof. Dr. Jehangir Bharucha, whose insightful discussions on personal finance matters have enriched my understanding and have been integrated into this book. The many hours spent in the college staff room with him, refining the templates for maintaining records, have been very productive.

I am grateful to Prof. Dr. (CA) Kishore Peshori, Principal of Smt. M. M. K. College, for his invaluable insights and rigorous review of the manuscript. His expertise greatly contributed to the refinement of this work.

I extend my heartfelt gratitude to Shri Khushro Bulsara, Head - BSE Investor Protection Fund, and his dedicated team for sharing their invaluable insights on Investor Awareness and Protection. Their knowledge greatly enriched the content of this book. I'm equally thankful to Kaiyomurz Daver, Head – Marketing, Bandhan AMC, and Ms. Mamtha Vaidya, Assistant Vice President - Marketing and Investor Education at AMFI, for their unwavering support and guidance. A special acknowledgement is due to Shri Yogesh Kundnani, Vice President - Business Development at CDSL, and Shri Sanjay Nunes, Assistant Manager at CDSL, for their invaluable contribution and expertise that have illuminated this endeavour.

I would like to express my sincere gratitude to the topmost functionaries of the Hyderabad (Sind) National Collegiate Board – The President, Shri Anil Harish, Former President and Trustee, Shri Kishu Mansukhani, and Dr. Niranjan Hiranandani, Provost, HSNC University, Mumbai, and Past President, H(S)NC Board, and the Trustees, Shri Lal Chellaram and Ms. Maya Shahani. They have tirelessly and consistently pursued and achieved goals and excellence in the educational landscape of Mumbai. Projects like mine have been inspired by their exemplary dedication to the cause of education.

My profound thankfulness goes out to Principal Dinesh Panjwani, Secretary of the H(S)NC Board and the Former and First Vice-Chancellor of HSNC University, Mumbai. His guidance has been invaluable in grooming me in academic administration and also instilling in me a process-driven approach in the pursuit of the establishment of viable and sustainable systems.

My sincere thanks to Dr. Hemlata Bagla, Vice-Chancellor, H(S)NC University, Mumbai, for fostering an environment that promotes growth and innovation.

To Dr. Pooja Ramchandani, my Principal, teachers, staff of H.R College of College & Economics, and my academic peers in various universities, colleges, and institutions, I owe a debt of gratitude for their constant love and support. Their dedication to education and commitment to nurturing a positive learning environment is testimony to their professionalism and passion.

I am thankful to my neighbour, Mr. Varun Rupani, who has authored numerous books on Graphology. His encouragement and experience in book publishing, which he generously shared with me, particularly his insights about Notion Press, were invaluable in my journey.

I extend my thanks to Kshitij Sharma, Joint Chairperson of the Placement Cell at H.R College for his diligent assistance in typing and researching and for his unwavering commitment to maintaining our timelines. His involvement was critical in ensuring the timely completion of this book.

My profound gratitude to Dr. Charanjeet Kaur, former Head of the Department of English, Smt. C.H.M. College, and Editorial Consultant, for her careful reading and astute insights regarding this book.

A sincere thanks to Notion Press and their dedicated staff for their prompt assistance with a second round of editing, DTP, typesetting, and cover design. Their professionalism and expertise greatly contributed to the fruition of this book. I appreciate Diya Chandhok, my publishing manager, for helping me publish my book.

In particular, I extend my deepest gratitude to Shri Nanik Rupani, Founder & Chairman Emeritus of Priyadarshni Academy & Member H(S) NC Board for his invaluable support and encouragement. His unwavering commitment to community service and his inspiring dedication to nurturing initiatives have been a guiding light in the journey of writing this book.

I am deeply grateful to CA Priti Savla for her unwavering encouragement and pivotal role in connecting stakeholders, which was crucial in writing this book.

And last but certainly not least, my profound thanks to my students, who are a constant source of inspiration. Their eagerness to learn, their thoughtful questions, and their resilience in the face of challenges remind me every day why I embarked on this journey.

It is to all these individuals and many others unnamed, who have contributed to this work in their own distinctive ways, that I dedicate my efforts.

Thank you.

Introduction

Life, invariably, presents us with crossroads that shape our identities. There have been six pivotal moments in my life that significantly moulded my passion for financial education and money management.

You might wonder why I've chosen to share these deeply personal experiences with you. Why not simply introduce the Wealth Diary and emphasise its significance? But, the narratives are fundamental to my purpose. They transcend simply delineating the 'how' – they underscore the 'why' behind our financial decisions. They personify the real-world implications of monetary decisions, making the often-esoteric ideas of financial education tangible and relatable.

This isn't a rags-to-riches tale or a manual on how to amass millions. It's about moments in an ordinary person's life, the lessons derived from them, and the wisdom passed down from my mother: "It is often wiser to learn from others' experiences than to start from scratch," she says. I invite my readers, first, to delve into the stories in Section I; if they resonate with you, you will want to proceed to Section II, which houses the Wealth Diary.

The power of storytelling became clear to me through an interaction with Krisha, my young daughter. Once, when I spoke to her, emphasizing the need for a regular exercise routine, she found my direct approach uninspiring, and I understood that a story-telling approach would be far more helpful. This exchange illuminated how discussions about finance can be tedious for many. Its profound importance becomes more comprehensible and compelling when narrated through vivid stories and life experiences, extracting insights, which I term 'life insights' or 'finance insights'. These insights often traverse beyond mere financial decisions, providing a holistic conception of our monetary choices, within the broader fabric of our existence.

As the term suggests, personal finance is deeply individualistic. While overarching principles, like the importance of savings or the perils of high-interest debt, are universally acknowledged, the detailed strategies can differ dramatically among individuals. Elements like income, personal values, aspirations, family dynamics, geographic location, and risk appetite profoundly influence one's financial blueprint: "What suits one may not fit another, or, it's not a one-size-fits-all approach." For instance, while some might view homeownership as pivotal for wealth creation, others might prioritise flexibility and choose to rent a house.

Some might emphasise a robust emergency fund, while others lean towards aggressive investments. This spectrum highlights the need for personalised financial guidance, recognising that there isn't a universal solution in money management. Personal finance is an inherently unique journey, tailored to the individual. Just as no two people are exactly alike, their financial situations and goals also vary significantly. Let's delve deeper into this fascinating realm of financial individuality.

Though personal finance is deeply individualistic, sharing personal experiences aims to spotlight those universal moments with which most can empathise. Life's rich mosaic encompasses events that, while unique in their nuances, often echo common themes. In unveiling my financial odyssey, I hope to touch upon those shared moments and many experiences, like grappling with the financial aspects of marriage, adapting to a newborn, and navigating through finances during unforeseen events like accidents, or the monetary shifts of career transitions.

These shared experiences, though varied in their specifics, strike a chord with many. This book isn't about presenting a cookie-cutter solution but about fostering a sense of solidarity and understanding in the intricate world of personal finance.

"In a manner reminiscent of a 'Janam Kundli,' Section II of this book can be likened to a celestial map of your wealth. Just as a 'Janam Kundli' intricately charts the positions of celestial bodies at the time of your birth, offering profound insights into your life's journey, strengths, and challenges, Section II serves as a financial diary—a systematic record meticulously detailing every facet of your wealth. This financial almanac, much like its astrological counterpart, holds the power to illuminate your financial path, offering invaluable insights into your assets, investments, debts, and more. Just as a 'Janam Kundli' guides one's life decisions, the Wealth Diary in Section II empowers you and your wealth manager to make informed financial choices, set meaningful goals, and plan for a prosperous financial future."

"The purpose of a storyteller is not to tell you how to think but to give you questions to think upon."

- Brandon Sanders

Section I

Chapter 1

"After Life"

My father, Mukesh Hariram Punjabi, was a well-known yet humble lecturer in the Commerce Department at Smt. M. M. P. Shah Women's College in Wadala, which is affiliated with SNDT Women's University. He was also the Special Executive Officer (SEO) for the Government of Maharashtra and a Member of the District Consumer Redressal Forum - those days commonly known as the Consumer Forum, as consumer protection was his passion.

My mother, Smt. Nisha Mukesh Punjabi came from a family with a business background; her father used to run a factory in Nashik, manufacturing cattle feed; so, she was not too inclined towards academics and studied till the XI Std., with great difficulty. My father continued to pursue his LLB even after my brother Manish and I were born, and our mother supported Dad in all his academic endeavours.

We were a happy-go-lucky, perfect family. I was in the XI Std. and Manish, who is two years younger than me, was in the IX Std. It was on 18 August 2000, a Thursday night when my father suddenly complained of chest pain and heaviness in his arms. My mother quickly called his father and brother Sunil, who stayed barely a kilometre away from our house. They arrived within 15 minutes, and we took him to the newly inaugurated heart specialty hospital, which was just eight buildings, precisely 350 metres away! (In those days, there were no Google Maps; today, we can calculate the distance and the average time - it would be just two minutes by car).

My father was unconscious, and in the hospital, he was put on a pacemaker (a device that helps a person's heartbeat at a normal rate and rhythm). We were stunned when the doctor declared that my father was no more. The whole world turned upside down for our family, for this was something we could never have imagined.

In the initial stages, our grandparents were our main support, and they took care of us. I, Manish, and my mother Nisha had no idea of what was going to happen! The loss of my father was irreparable, and as the eldest son of the family, my grandfather always told me it was my duty to pull myself together and keep the family united and strong.

After a few months of mourning, we all had to face the harsh facts - what about the finances?! Who would pay the bills? My father was in a grant-in-aid job. So, this job had a family pension scheme; however, getting the family pension sometimes could take its own time, sometimes, even years! And my mother had no clue about how the pension system worked.

Many questions assailed us:

- Can my Mom access my father's salary account?
- Who is the nominee in that account? What is the process to get this amount after his death?
- Did my father make a Will? If yes, who has it, and where is it?
- What kind of investments are there? Only FD's, Mutual Funds, Shares, etc., or are there any other assets?
- Which bank is the locker in? Is that the only locker?

  So many questions...

Then, a most unexpected thing happened when one of my Dad's colleagues came home to offer his condolences and handed my Mom a check of rupees two lakhs; my Mom was in tears, feeling grateful that my father had such good friends and colleagues who repaid their debts they owed him in our time of need!

However, too, I was in tears, but for a different reason. I wondered how many more such friends and colleagues were there who had borrowed from my father and probably had no intention of repaying us!

That was the first time I sat down with my mother and asked her to take out all the papers in my father's cupboard and a maroon briefcase which he always carried with him to work. The briefcase had a number lock that could be unlocked by rolling the four digits to reach the correct combination. My Mom used to open that bag every day, and she knew the passcode for the briefcase; however, she was so stressed that she was struggling to remember it. After many attempts, she managed to recall it and open the bag. She apologised to us and grew tearful as memories of my father flashed in front of her eyes. She made a very important statement that time when she said, "I wish I had written this passcode somewhere. I have always known it, but today, because of the stress, I simply could not remember it."

I realised that my father was extremely systematic in everything he did. For example, he was passionate about photography and he noted down the names of the people along with the date, time, and place of each photograph in the family albums. His maroon pocket telephone directory contained not only telephone numbers but also the code to his maroon briefcase.

In the not-so-distant past, the times I fondly refer to as 'BM' – 'Before Mobile Phones' – our minds were the sacred repositories of phone numbers, addresses, birthdays, and so many other nuggets of information. We relied on our memory, which was almost like an internal, biological directory. In those BM days, remembering phone numbers was not just necessary; it was a skill, a matter of pride. I recall how some of my cousins were affectionately called 'telephone directories' because they could rattle off the phone numbers of even distant relatives at a moment's notice.

Fast forward to today, and our smartphones have become our second brains. These sleek devices, always at our fingertips, store more than just phone numbers. They are our navigators, our librarians, our personal assistants, and our external memory banks. Our reliable devices remember our appointments, direct us to our destinations, and even prompt us to send birthday wishes to family and friends. The convenience is undeniable and, in many ways, empowering.

However, this convenience comes at a subtle cost. I find it a bit ironic that while our phones get smarter, certain aspects of our memory seem to be getting a bit, well, lazier. Can I recite my best friend's phone number, or my boss's, from memory? I doubt it. Today, if I am asked for a close family member's number in an emergency and my phone battery is dead, I would find myself in a tough spot.

This dependence on technology, while incredibly useful, sometimes makes me wonder if we are underutilising the true potential of our memory. It is as if our mental muscles for memorisation are not being exercised as they once were. Instead of remembering, we are outsourcing this fundamental human skill to our devices. We are, in essence, 'offloading' our memory to the Cloud.

But this isn't about demonising technology. Smartphones and the internet have brought the world closer than we could have ever imagined in the BM era. They have made our lives richer and more convenient in countless ways. The question is about balance and mindfulness – about using technology to enhance our human capabilities, not inadvertently diminish them. Are we losing something essential and deeply human when we outsource our remembering to a device? Or are we, on the other hand, freeing our minds to focus on higher-order thinking, creativity, and problem-solving, unburdened by the need to remember data that can be easily stored and retrieved?

These are the questions that our digital age poses, and they are worth pondering as we navigate this extraordinary era of human history. Technology should be our tool, not our crutch, and striking that balance is one of the defining challenges of our time.

In the BM age, life was simpler in many ways, yet laden with its own complexities. I vividly remember how efficiently my mother managed household affairs, her memory sharp as a tack. She knew where the chequebooks were kept, which bank she needed to visit to access the locker for her jewellery, and the specifics of various bank accounts. And yet, despite this comprehensive awareness, there wasn't a systematic record of all such financial matters.

My mother, like many women of her generation, deferred financial matters to my father. "Aap hai na, plz dekh lo, mere palle nahi padta hai ye sab," she would say – a Hindi phrase meaning, "You are here to look after these matters; I don't understand them." She operated under the belief that my father would always be around to handle the finances. In her worldview, financial management was his responsibility, and she comfortably stayed away from those conversations, focusing her energies on other aspects of family life.

My father, on the other hand, was meticulous in his own way. His wisdom led him to record essential information in a small maroon telephone directory. That humble notebook, not much to look at but rich with information, suddenly became our "Yellow Pages." In times of doubt or crisis, that maroon directory was our go-to, our lifeline. It was the repository of knowledge that held the family's financial world together.

Times have changed, and the dynamics within families are shifting. In today's world, it is increasingly important for all members of a household to have a working understanding of their finances. As I reflect on my parents' approach, I am very fortunate to realise the inherent risks in leaving all financial knowledge and responsibility to one person.

This reflection isn't a critique of my parents' choices; it was a common approach in their time, shaped by the cultural and societal norms of the BM era. However, it serves as a stark reminder to us, living in a different time, of the need for financial literacy to be a shared responsibility in a family.

In today's complex, fast-paced world, where economic stability can be elusive, understanding and managing finances is a crucial skill—not just for the 'man of the house' but for everyone. Women, too, need to be equal partners in this domain, not just for their empowerment but for the overall security and well-being of the family. As we move forward, let us break the cycle and ensure that financial literacy is not seen as the domain of one gender or the other, but a shared responsibility, a common language spoken and understood by all members of the family. Let the maroon telephone directory of the past remind us that knowledge should not be held in one pair of hands but shared and understood by all who are a part of the family's journey.

My father's death was a turning point in my life, and I decided to learn about personal finances, and money matters, and make finance a part of dinner table conversations in the family.

Life Insights: Open and honest discussions about wealth and investments are vital in a couple's relationship for several reasons, as follows:

1. **Financial Goals Alignment:** Every individual has his/her own financial goals and ways of managing money. Couples should discuss and align their financial objectives, be it for buying a house, saving for retirement, investing in a business, planning for a vacation, or managing debt. This alignment helps in crafting a joint financial strategy and fosters co-operation in financial decision-making.
2. **Shared Responsibility:** Money management is a shared responsibility. When both partners are involved in financial discussions and decisions, it can lead to more balanced and holistic financial planning. It can also reduce the burden on one person and prevent misunderstandings or resentment.
3. **Risk Management:** Discussing wealth and investment matters allows couples to understand each other's risk tolerance. Some might be conservative investors, preferring secure, low-risk options, while others might be comfortable taking bigger financial risks for potentially higher returns. Understanding these differences is the key to making joint investment decisions that satisfy both partners.
4. **Emergency Planning:** Life is unpredictable, and having a solid financial plan can provide security in case of unexpected events, like job loss, illness, or other emergencies. When couples discuss their finances, they can jointly develop an emergency fund and an insurance strategy.
5. **Securing the Future:** Especially for couples planning to have children or retire together, conversations about savings, investments, retirement funds, and estate planning are crucial. This ensures the future financial well-being of the family and makes the transition into retirement easier.
6. **Fostering Trust and Transparency:** Open conversations about money can prevent financial infidelity, where one partner hides financial information from the other. It encourages trust, transparency, and understanding in the relationship.

Remember, financial matters can be a sensitive topic for many couples. However, having regular, open, and respectful conversations about money can greatly strengthen a relationship and help build a secure financial future together.

Most of us think of money, wealth, and assets as things that concern us only during our own lifetime. The first chapter is significantly titled 'After Life' because I was lucky enough to realise, when I was only sixteen, that wealth is like a family name—a legacy handed down from generation to generation. So, one has to plan and decide for the surviving members or the future generation—whether it be in the form of nominations, preparing and registering a Will, or creating a Trust.

1. There are many questions that would arise in your mind now:
2. Does a Will supersede a nomination or does a nomination supersede a Will?
3. In case a person dies intestate (without a Will), who is a successor?
4. Do your parents have insurance on their premium credit card?
5. Have they taken any Online Term Plan or Personal Accident Cover?
6. What happens to my HUF after my death?

The aim of this book is different, but I will surely address these questions in my next book; for now, let us concentrate on the issues raised so far.

In our cultural fabric, there exists a poignant, heartfelt prayer of many Indian women: that they should depart from this world before their husbands. Raised within this cultural framework, my mother was no different. She lived with the unspoken conviction that my father would be her companion for the entire duration of her life and that he would outlive her. This is not just a sentimental wish. It is a prayer deeply rooted in our cultural narrative, where the thought of a woman living without her husband is often accompanied by societal discomfort and perceived vulnerability.

"But death," as the saying goes, "is the great equaliser." It is the only certainty in our uncertain lives. And, as my mother's story underscores, the timing of our exit from this world is the greatest unknown factor. We don't get to choose who goes first in a partnership. This is a harsh reality but a reality, nonetheless, which one has to accept.

My mother's approach was not unique; it is mirrored in countless households across our country, and it serves as a profound lesson for all of us. Regardless of the emotional bonds and the prayers we offer, we need to come to terms with life's fundamental uncertainties.

Understanding this, it becomes imperative for both partners in a relationship to be well-versed in financial matters. It's not just about bills and account numbers; it's about security, autonomy, and preparedness for the unknown chapters of life.

A conscious effort to familiarise oneself with the household's finances is not an act of mistrust or a challenge to traditional roles within a family. It is a practical, empowering, and loving step to ensure that both partners are equipped to navigate life's path, however winding it may be, with confidence and security.

So, let this be a heartfelt appeal to all — not just as a matter of practicality, but as a gesture of deep love and respect for our partners: engage in open, honest, and regular discussions about money with your spouse or a trusted, loved one. Make it a point to know where important documents are kept, understand the investments that have been made, and be aware of the debts and assets that are a part of your shared life.

In doing so, we honour not just our own lives, but the lives of those we hold dearest. We create a space where transparency reigns, and where the spectre of the unknown loses some of its power to induce fear and anxiety. Let us rewrite the narrative. In our bonds of love and partnership, let us find not just emotional but also financial strength and security, affirming that we are, in every sense, true partners on this journey of life.

Personal finance is about more than just saving and investing; it's about savouring the fruits of your hard work and pampering yourself along the way. However, the lessons from this chapter can be summarised in a quote: 'Live as if you were to die tomorrow, plan as if you were to live forever.' This quote beautifully encapsulates the essence of balancing the present and the future. While you enjoy the present, it is crucial to remember there is a future to take care of too.

It urges us not to hold back when it comes to using our resources to enrich our lives and embrace experiences because life's unpredictability reminds us to live it to the fullest. Yet, it also highlights the importance of forward-thinking, financial planning, encouraging us to adopt a long-term perspective on our finances.

This planning includes saving for retirement, investing wisely, setting up emergency funds, and ensuring we have the appropriate insurance in place. But it doesn't stop at our retirement. It also involves estate planning and leaving a financial legacy so that our loved ones are taken care of even after we are gone. It is about planning for life, death, and everything in between, giving equal importance to living fully in the present and preparing for the future.

"Seeing death as the end of life is like seeing the horizon as the end of the ocean."

– David Searls

Chapter 2

"The Black Swan Event": Understanding the Financial Implications of an Emergency

The second chapter is titled 'Black Swan Event.' A "Black Swan" event is a term used in the world of finance to describe an extremely negative event or occurrence that is impossibly difficult to predict. The term was popularised by finance professor, writer, and former Wall Street trader Nassim Nicholas Taleb.

Black Swan events are typically characterised by their extreme rarity and severe impact. These events can cause catastrophic damage to an economy, and they can't be predicted using standard forecasting tools.

Examples of Black Swan events include the 2008 financial crash, the dotcom crisis of 2000, the COVID-19 pandemic, and natural disasters like tsunamis and earthquakes. The main idea is that while these events are almost impossible to predict, they have a significant and often lasting impact.

The term is frequently used in discussions of financial market risks, and it serves as a reminder that past performance is not necessarily indicative of future results. That is why financial analysts and risk managers try to plan for the unforeseen, including Black Swan events when they build models and make forecasts.

The second incident that shaped my life was when I was recruited as a Management Trainee in the Financial Planning Group of Kotak

Securities as the Relationship Manager, where I had to meet and advise High Networth Individuals (HNIs) on their investment portfolio. I was lucky to get good teachers and mentors, the knowledge and skills I had gained in my undergraduate & post-graduation helped me become a good Relationship Manager; my clients loved me and fortunately, they valued my advice. I was very happily placed, and life seemed to be on a roll. Then, one day in August 2006, my family and I set out for my cousin's place in Bandra for Ganpati Darshan. For that special day, my mother made a trip to her bank's locker and adorned herself with her cherished vintage jewellery. My grandfather was driving the car, and due to overheating, we had parked the car on the side with the parking lights on. Suddenly, out of nowhere, a Tata Sumo rammed into our car, and I suffered a blackout. When I regained consciousness, I realised that my brother had a head injury, and my mother, with all her fancy jewellery, was lying unconscious on the road.

This accident made me realise the importance of knowing about first aid in life. With no experience in administering first aid, I was unable to move my leg or get up; I could only helplessly look on as my unconscious mother was being pulled out of the car while people stared at her jewellery. I also heard people murmur that, being a motor accident, it was a police case. They warned each other, "Don't touch, fukat mein hum fas jayenge." People in those days feared police procedures and questioning involved with a motor accident and would refrain from being party to any such incident, even if it involved helping someone in need; so help at that moment seemed difficult to come by. On the other hand, thanks to the knowledge gained from watching both Bollywood and Hollywood movies, I realised the importance of keeping my brother awake. He had suffered a head injury and was bleeding so profusely that I could not even make out whether he was injured on the forehead or on the back of his head.

In the midst of all this, there was a Honda CRV Car (I don't exactly recollect the colour but think it was white), and from it, - I can only describe him as such - an angel alighted and came up to me and whispered in my ear, "Son, don't worry we are with you." I clearly remember how, throughout the time, I was shaking my brother anxiously, in order to keep him awake, I was fervently praying to God to help me somehow to take my Mom, brother, grandmother, and grandfather to the doctor. Unlike my mother, my grandfather and grandmother were conscious and could walk with support. Our 'angel' told me that first he would take my mother and my grandparents to Lilavati Hospital, as it was nearby, and after that, he would come back for my brother and me.

In the meantime, I desperately struggled to keep my brother awake because, thanks to a steady diet of Bollywood movies, I was terribly afraid of him slipping into a coma. However, within no time, our 'angel' returned to the accident site, took my brother and me in his Honda CRV, and said, "Don't worry, your family is in good hands."

I had my visiting card in my pocket and a Kotak Bank Debit card. Coming from a Sindhi family, I had acquired the habit of saving pretty early, and it being only six months since I had joined, most of my salary was in my savings account. During the whole ride, I felt tremendous gratitude towards this 'angelic' couple who were taking so much trouble for us strangers. I tried to assure them that they would not get into any trouble with the police, was about to give my debit card and said, "Whatever the expenses, please save my family... I have the money." Even before I could finish speaking, I heard the voices of ward boys, nurses, and doctors, and I was in the Emergency Trauma Care Ward.

As filmy as it may sound, I asked the doctor to call the God-sent angel and I told him, "I don't even know your name. Once my family is okay, I would love to come and meet you and thank you for what not many people would have done!" He urged me in a kind voice to focus on my health and family and slipped his visiting card into my shirt's pocket.

At this moment, the doctor came and asked us many questions like:

- What medicines have you taken? I could answer for myself; however, I did not know what medicines my mother was on.
- Do you smoke? When was the last time you smoked?
- Do you consume alcohol? How many units, and how frequently?
- Any allergies to food or medicines?
- Any family history of diabetes, blood pressure, or coronary heart diseases?

Then came the financial questions:

- Do you have any Mediclaim and health insurance? Can you call your Third-Party Administrator (TPA) for authorization?
- We need a copy of your health insurance policy, and do you have any pre-existing illnesses?

These questions made me realise that every family should have some emergency money; it could be cash or liquid money in a Savings/Current bank account or a sweep in FD which can be closed prematurely from an ATM on withdrawal.

Well, I have not forgotten about my 'angel' who left his visiting card in my shirt pocket. The card was transferred to the safety of my wallet, and I found a name for the face. My 'angel' was Mr. K. Ramkumar, Group Head, HR, ICICI Bank; later on in his career, he took charge as Executive Director on the Board of ICICI Bank. He was on the Boards of ICICI Prudential Life Insurance and ICICI Ventures. Prior to his retirement, he was the President of ICICI Foundation, ICICI Groups, CSR arm. Now, he is a co-founder of the Leadership Centre.

A top executive from the Board of a leading Private Sector bank in the country, and yet with such humility and humanity that he came to the rescue of an unknown family! I can't thank him enough in this lifetime...!

I had medical insurance from Kotak Securities which got exhausted; it was a group Mediclaim provided to all employees. Then, we had to use our personal Mediclaim policy from another company. Kirti Motwani, my aunt who is an Insurance Consultant, helped us understand how to claim from both the insurance companies—the group insurance Mediclaim amount provided by my employers and my personal Mediclaim policy.

I will tell you more about the role of Kirti Aunty in the subsequent chapter. For now, the insights and relevant questions are:

Financial Insight: Should you have a personal Mediclaim policy despite having a group Mediclaim policy?

Having your personal Mediclaim policy in addition to a company group Mediclaim policy can provide numerous advantages. Here are some reasons why it can be beneficial:

1. **Coverage after Employment Ends:** Your employer's group Mediclaim policy will cover you only as long as you are employed with the company. If you leave the company, retire, or are terminated, you could be left without health insurance. A personal Mediclaim policy will provide uninterrupted coverage, regardless of your employment status.
2. **Inadequate Coverage:** Sometimes, the coverage provided by the employer might not be adequate to meet your specific health needs. A personal Mediclaim policy allows you to customise the coverage based on your health requirements, age, family medical history, and lifestyle factors.
3. **Family Coverage:** While some employers may offer coverage for your dependents, not all do. A personal Mediclaim policy can ensure that all your family members are adequately covered.
4. **Waiting Periods for Pre-existing Diseases:** Group health insurance policies typically cover pre-existing diseases immediately or after a short waiting period, while personal policies might require a longer waiting period. If you switch jobs and hence, insurers, you might need to serve this waiting period before getting coverage for pre-existing conditions. Having a personal policy in parallel helps negate this risk.
5. **Policy Continuity:** Employers may change health insurance providers, which could affect your continuity benefits. If you have a personal health insurance policy, you don't have to worry about losing these benefits.
6. **Added Benefits:** Personal Mediclaim policies may offer additional benefits that your group policy doesn't. This could include things like maternity coverage, mental health coverage, alternative treatments, and higher room rent limits, among others.
7. **Post-Retirement Coverage:** After retirement, getting a new health insurance policy can be difficult and expensive due to age and possible pre-existing conditions. A personal Mediclaim policy taken earlier can provide a safety net in your golden years when healthcare needs are likely to be high.

The probability of such an event happening in anyone's life is very low however, it's not zero. I pray that no one should face any Black Swan event, hence it's best not to reinvent the wheel. The main takeaways from this chapter are threefold:

1. **Wealth Management Perspective:** Having emergency funds and comprehensive health insurance is absolutely crucial. Emergencies are unexpected and can strike at any time, leaving you in a financial crisis if you are not prepared. It is important to plan ahead, ensuring there is an emergency fund that can cover at least 3-6 months of expenses and a comprehensive health insurance plan that covers various aspects, including hospitalisation, medicines, and other medical needs.
2. **Knowledge of Medical History:** Being aware of your family's medical history and current medications is often overlooked, but it is incredibly important. This knowledge can be a lifesaver in medical emergencies. Knowing the details of any ongoing treatment or medication could help the medical team provide appropriate and timely care.
3. **Personal Empathy and Humanity:** The act of stepping in to help others, as demonstrated by Mr. Ramkumar, embodies empathy and humanity at its best. Life's unpredictability means that we may find ourselves in need of help someday. Therefore, it is equally important to be willing to extend that help to others when they are in need.

These threefold lessons underscore the importance of financial preparedness, medical knowledge, and personal empathy, and readiness to help others during unexpected events. They serve as important reminders that while we cannot control life's unforeseen events, we can control how we respond to them, and that preparedness, knowledge, and compassion are keys to dealing with such events effectively.

"The inability to predict outliers implies the inability to predict the course of history."

– Nassim Nicholas Taleb,
The Black Swan: The Impact of the Highly Improbable

Chapter 3

Career Pivots: From Industry to Academia and its Financial Implications and Preparations

The third incident that moulded my life and my perspective toward money was undoubtedly the most challenging one. The situation demanded a decision that ran counter to popular opinion, advice from well-wishers, and even my own inner predilections.

I began my career as a Management Trainee at Kotak Securities, in a campus recruitment drive. The highlight of my role was the rich heterogeneity of people I interacted with, spanning across various walks of life. This included businessmen, start-up enthusiasts, professionals, bureaucrats, service staff, freelancers, Bollywood personalities - virtually every kind of professional you could name. My core responsibility was to pursue individuals with significant financial resources and persuade them to invest with us across various asset classes, tailored to their risk preferences.

This role provided me with invaluable insights into not just individual financial behaviour, but also familial financial dynamics. I gained an understanding of their financial perspectives, their attitudes toward money, and their broader financial ambitions. The generosity and kindness of these clients never ceased to amaze me. Some treated me like an extension of their own family, so much so that even after a gap of 14 years from the industry, I found myself invited to family events like the wedding of a daughter. This very same daughter is now a teacher and holds a special place in my family's heart.

Following this, I had the privilege of joining DBS Bank (Development Bank of Singapore) for a brief period. Professionally, I felt fulfilled, yet there was an underlying unrest though I could not exactly pinpoint what it was. Fortune smiled on me, I was teaching at my alma mater Tolani College of Commerce & Economics there I had the opportunity to meet my current Principal Prof. (Dr.) Pooja Ramchandani, who introduced me to the Sheriff of Mumbai and the Principal of H. R. College, Dr. (Mrs.) Indu Shahani. She posed a straightforward but profound question to me: "What do you genuinely aspire for in life, young man? While you can always return to selling financial products, I invite you to join me on this academic journey. Trust me, you won't regret it. Once, I stood at a similar crossroads, choosing between teaching and selling soaps. Now, it is your turn to decide."

Inherently, I've always been an explorer. With my father being a teacher, my grandfather serving as a trustee at CBM High School, Koliwada (under the aegis of the Hinduja Group), and my mother transitioning into computer education post his demise, academia had always woven itself into our familial fabric. So, when Dr. Shahani extended an invitation to dive into the academic world, I felt a compelling urge to accept.

Transitioning to academia felt like stepping into an entirely different universe compared to the corporate sector. It was a "Career Pivot." A career pivot is a significant shift in one's career trajectory. In such a move, an individual transitions from his/her current profession or role to one that is often distinctly different. This shift might encompass changes in job function, industry, or both. However, unlike a complete career change where one starts anew, a career pivot typically leverages the skills, knowledge, and experiences acquired in the previous role but applies them in a fresh context.

You might wonder why I refer to this as a 'career pivot' rather than a career change. This will become clearer in the concluding chapter, where all the dots connect. But for now, let us backtrack to 2009. During this period, equity penetration was notably low, and it remains so even today. My role in wealth management was primarily centred on elucidating the benefits and challenges of the Securities Markets in India and discussing the risks linked to various asset classes.

Upon entering the academic world, I served as a full-time teacher for the B.Com programme. According to the Maharashtra Government's stipulated workload, I was charged with teaching Commerce subjects, like Principles of Management and Advertising. However, my then Vice-Principal, Prof. Heena Thakkar recognised my expertise. She entrusted me with modules on financial market subjects, like Mutual Fund Management, Regulation in the Securities Market, Wealth Management, Risk Management, Innovations in Banking and Insurance, Personal Finance, and more. Teaching subjects that mirrored my professional journey felt natural. This real-world experience made me a favourite among students, as I often incorporated practical scenarios into lectures and organised seminars featuring industry experts.

In retrospect, transitioning to teaching was a logical step in my career. But at what price? I had to initially accept a pay reduction of close to 75% to pursue my passion until my approval came from the University, and my salary was released as per the pay scales by the office of the Joint Director, Higher Education. However, even the salary as per scale was much lower than my current corporate salary. My last drawn salary surpassed the college Principal's, the top academic and administrative position in any educational institution. It sounds almost irrational, doesn't it?

My prospective mother-in-law certainly thought so. She was taken aback at my decision, remarking, "I can understand your shift from being a stockbroker to a banker with an increased salary. But transitioning to a professorship with a pay cut? How do you plan to support your family? I'm not convinced it is a prudent choice."

I vividly remember that heartfelt moment with my fiancée, Diya. Tears streamed down her face as she passionately told her mother, "I believe in him with all my heart, Mom! Even if he doesn't earn a penny, I know he'll care for me. We'll find our happiness, come what may!" It felt like a scene right out of a Bollywood film. Embracing the classic sentiment, 'kabhi kabhi pagalpan bhi zaroori hai (Sometimes, a touch of madness is essential),' she took a brave leap of faith. Going against societal expectations, we began our shared journey and, in time, celebrated our union, bearing witness to our unyielding love and trust.

Life Insights:

In the vast tapestry of life, each individual is granted a singular, fleeting life. This life, with its myriad experiences, choices, and paths, is a one-time gift. Among the various decisions we make, our career choices stand out as some of the most defining. After all, we spend a significant portion of our lives working, striving, and building within our chosen professions.

The phrase, 'you have just one life,' is not just a casual reminder of our mortality but a profound nudge to live authentically. In the realm of careers, this means pursuing a path that resonates with your core values, passions, and aspirations. It is about not settling for a job merely because that is what is expected or because it's a safe choice. Instead, it is about carving out a niche for yourself in a field you genuinely care about, where Mondays are welcomed with enthusiasm, and challenges are seen as invigorating puzzles waiting to be solved.

But why is it so crucial to live the career of your choice? Firstly, when you are engaged in a profession that aligns with your interests, the likelihood of experiencing burnout decreases. You are more motivated, more committed, and often, more successful. Moreover, a career that resonates with you often translates into better mental health, personal satisfaction, and a more balanced life.

Yet, making such a choice is not always a straightforward decision. Societal pressures, financial obligations, and even personal insecurities can sometimes cloud judgement, pushing us towards careers that might not be the best fit for us. But it is essential to remember that while external factors are transient, the regret of not following one's passion can linger.

This narrative is not to highlight the right career moves but to highlight the financial, emotional and strategic long-term implications associated with any career pivot and one's sensitivity and preparedness for the same.

In conclusion, as you navigate the journey of life, remember that your career is not just about earning a paycheck. It is a significant portion of your life's story, a testament to your skills, passions, and legacy. Embrace it wholeheartedly, choose wisely, and remember: you have one life. Make it count by living the career of your choice.

Finance Insights:

A career pivot, while often driven by a desire for personal fulfilment or new challenges, carries with it both emotional and monetary implications. These aspects are intricately intertwined, shaping one's overall experience and perception of the transition.

Emotional Financial Implications:

1. **Anticipation and Uncertainty:** The thrill of diving into a new career can be overshadowed by the unpredictability of income. Will the new role provide the same level of financial stability? Such concerns can bring about anxiety and self-doubt.
2. **Comparative Earnings:** Especially if peers remain in the original field, there might be emotional stress tied to potential differences in earnings. "Am I earning enough?" can be a recurrent thought.
3. **Reaffirming Worth:** Pricing one's skills in a new market, especially if transitioning to freelance or consultancy roles, can be emotionally taxing. Determining what to charge clients or what salary to ask for requires reaffirming one's professional value.
4. **Investment in Self:** The emotional reward of investing in oneself, be it through further education or skill development, can be immense. However, the financial strain it sometimes brings can weigh on one's mind.

Monetary Financial Implications:

1. **Immediate Income Disruption:** A Career Pivot may lead to a temporary gap in earnings, especially if there is a break between jobs or the starting salary in a new field is lower.
2. **Training and Re-skilling:** Pivoting might necessitate undertaking new courses or certifications, representing a direct financial outlay.
3. **Benefit Adjustments:** Health insurance, retirement contributions, bonuses, and other perks might differ in the new role, impacting one's financial planning.
4. **Long-term Earning Potential:** A Career Pivot can change the trajectory of one's earning potential. The new career might have a different growth rate or salary cap.
5. **Lifestyle Adjustments:** Depending on the financial outcomes of the Pivot, one might need to modify one's spending habits, at least temporarily.

Understanding the emotional and monetary facets of a career pivot is crucial. While the emotional aspect revolves around feelings, perceptions, and self-worth, the monetary side is tangible, impacting daily life and future plans. By being cognizant of both these realms, one can make informed, balanced decisions, ensuring that the career transition is both personally fulfilling and financially viable.

Most of us may want to change our career or take up entrepreneurship; after all, it is the era of OTT and Start-up TV shows, and every kid on the block is looking for valuation.

In the intricate dance of life, our careers play a pivotal role in defining our rhythm. This chapter illuminates the emotional and financial ramifications that career choices, especially significant ones like a career pivot, can present. Each step, each decision, is a note that contributes to the melody of our life's song.

From a life perspective, the aim is clear: to lead a life of authenticity, passion, and alignment. We are encouraged to recognise the profound impact our professional choices can have on our overall happiness and well-being. The true measure of success is not just financial gain but also satisfaction, growth, and the legacy we leave behind. It is a call to action, to live deliberately and to make choices that resonate deeply with our core selves.

From a financial standpoint, the chapter delves deep into the intricate relationship between the heart and the wallet. Every career pivot is not just an emotional journey but a financial one. While the allure of a new beginning, like those painted in entrepreneurship and start-up shows, captivates many, it is important to tread with both excitement and caution. It is about understanding that while the heart has its dreams, the realities of life require careful planning and consideration.

In short, whether you're drawn to the clarion call of entrepreneurship, considering a significant career shift, or just evaluating your current path, remember this: life and finances are two sides of the same coin. To truly thrive, one must not only follow one's passion but do so with a clear understanding of its financial implications. As you stand at the crossroads, let your heart guide you, but arm yourself with knowledge to ensure that the path you choose is not just fulfilling but sustainable. After all, in the journey of life, the voyage is as important as the destination itself.

Chapter 4

"From 'I Do' to Bills Due": The Costly affair of Marriage

The fourth phenomenon that changed my life was marriage! Don't get me wrong! It changed my life for the better - and for good! I got married to my college sweetheart, Heena Shewakramani (Diya N. Punjabi, after marriage), and yes, she was there for me and my family all the time during our recovery from the accident. She had seen me on the hospital bed injured and confused with all the Mediclaim documents around me, and we used to wonder how our family would sail through this emergency.

We were happily married in December 2009, and life was going great; Diya's journey, right from her childhood, has been one of perseverance and resilience. Growing up without the presence of her father, whom she tragically lost when she was just a three-year-old, she was nurtured and brought up by her indomitable mother, who faced countless hardships courageously. Her cousins Raju and Janvi played a very significant role in getting us married. Our quintessential Indian wedding, with all its grandeur and celebrations, inevitably burned a significant hole in both our families' pockets. Yet, through this entire process, I learned a profound lesson: no matter how hard you try, no matter how much effort you put in, or no matter how genuine your intentions are, there will always be someone or the other who will remain discontented - be it family, friends, or colleagues.

We got married in Bollywood style; I thought we would be married by taking saath pheres (seven circumambulations around the holy fire), but that day I realised that in our Sindhi community, it is with chaar pheres and seven vows i.e. saath vachan that the marriage is solemnised. We both were excited that we would have to take seven rounds around the holy fire! We both didn't speak a word while the priest was reciting the prayers; however, our eyes communicated our ignorance, and we found our ignorance hilarious!

Be it during the marriage or after marriage, traditionally, there is always a huge discomfort in the families of the bride and the bridegroom about who would foot what portion of the bills; and this has to be handled without hurting the feelings of either family or violating any of the customs or traditions!

Life Insights:

Clearing the Fog: The Importance of Transparency in Wedding Finances.

It is clear that transparency and clarity in financial matters related to wedding ceremonies can significantly impact the well-being of couples and their families. This is necessary for the following reasons:

1. **Prevention of Misunderstandings:** Understanding who will bear what percentage of the wedding costs can prevent future misunderstandings and disputes. Clarity in the initial stages of the preparations can ensure that all parties are on the same page regarding their respective contributions.
2. **Financial Planning:** The cost of a wedding can be enormous. If families know their financial obligations in advance, they can plan accordingly. This may involve saving, budgeting, or adjusting their financial plans to accommodate the costs.
3. **Reduction of Stress:** Weddings can be stressful, particularly when there is uncertainty about who will pay for what. Clear communication about financial responsibilities can reduce this stress and allow everyone to enjoy the festivities.
4. **Avoiding the Debt Trap:** If not properly planned, the cost of a wedding can lead to significant debts. Knowing the costs upfront can

help families avoid taking on more financial responsibility than they can handle.

5. **Respect for Traditions:** Every culture has different traditions and customs associated with weddings, each with its own set of expenses. Understanding these traditions and who, traditionally, pays for what can help one to respect and uphold these customs, while ensuring that none of the parties involved is financially stressed.
6. **Start on a Solid Foundation:** For couples, understanding and planning for the financial aspects of their wedding can set a solid foundation for their future together. It can foster necessary conversations about money, spending habits, financial responsibilities, and future planning - all critical components of a healthy financial life together.

But well, financial decisions don't end with marriage. In fact, marriage brings greater financial responsibilities! Some of the questions that couples may have to answer mutually are:

1. How will we handle our bank accounts - Single, Joint, either/or, or survivor?
2. What are our individual and collective financial goals?
3. How much can each of us spend without the need to consult the other?
4. How much of our income will we save, and what savings goals do we have?
5. What are our attitudes towards lending money to friends or family?
6. How will we handle investment decisions? And who calls the shots?
7. When will we be financially prepared to start a family?

   And so on and so forth. Hmm…abhi to party shuru hui hai!

I must confess that after our marriage, our frequent disagreements and occasional arguments centred more on our attitudes toward money rather than on the actual expenditure itself. Our school and college curricula must have a module on 'couples and money' which brings such finance concepts to class with real world case studies.

In most couples, there is a communication gap regarding attitudes towards money. According to a poll of more than 1,300 Americans, couples who regularly talk about money—as often as once a week—are happier in their relationship than those who discuss finances less frequently. On the other hand, money is a source of conflict for nearly one-third of all couples, and even more so during stressful times—and any uncertainty about finances can add to that stress. Additional research from North Carolina State University suggests that working as a team and becoming financially literate can help.

So as a couple, we were no different and fell into the majority who discussed less about finances initially, and there was a gap. This communication gap became a primary source of our problems, prompting us to address certain questions that arose in our daily lives.

For instance, Diya has a penchant for shopping. Should she be free to buy a new dress whenever she wanted to, or should we establish some guidelines? Like purchasing dresses only for significant events or limiting it to once in three months?

Similarly, should there be guidelines for my expenses, too? For example, should I get a new phone merely because a newer model has been released, or should I continue using my current one for at least three years, provided it is in good working condition?

We both realised that discussing our spending and investment plans openly smoothed out many of the fault lines and deepened our understanding of each other. However, life isn't merely about adhering to rules. While we had set guidelines, we also indulged in surprising each other with gifts and granted each other the autonomy to make individual decisions.

Let us not forget that we both took significant risks: I left a lucrative banking career to embrace academia, accepting a significant pay cut. Meanwhile, she chose to marry me when my income had dwindled. A pressing concern was how we would manage our dues. We recognised that to achieve our broader aspirations, it was imperative for both of us to work and earn. Seeking my advice, and with my extensive reading on entrepreneurship, combined with the security of my government job, I could provide her with a safety net, allowing her to take risks and venture into wealth creation. With the support of my former student, Mr. Viraj Singal, she established a capacity-building training organisation to bridge the industry-academia divide. The unwavering support I received from Diya during these times was extraordinary, and I'll be grateful to her forever, for the way she stood by me. Diya's financial contributions were instrumental in allowing me to focus on my academic pursuits, without the constant worry of meeting financial obligations.

I had once believed that my professional relationship with money and investments had ended and that my future lay solely in the chalk-and-board classrooms. I imagined students looking up to me as a "sage on the stage," though I actually aimed to be a "guide by the side." But, I recalled the words of my first boss at Kotak Securities, Mr. B. Gopkumar, who was an invaluable mentor during that phase: "Punjabi, you can leave the market (Securities Market), but the market will never leave you," he had stated. At the time, I couldn't grasp the depth of his words, but I had already made my choice - the transition to academia, despite the financial setbacks involved.

Life Insights:

I can affirm that going through a career change, especially one that involves a pay cut, can be a challenging and, sometimes, an overwhelming transition. During this period, the support of your spouse and other family members becomes indispensable for several reasons:

1. **Emotional Stability:** A career change, coupled with a pay cut, can often lead to heightened stress and anxiety. It is a time when one might doubt one's decisions, capabilities, or future prospects. The emotional support, reassurance, and encouragement of a spouse can provide the much-needed stability and confidence during this period.
2. **Shared Financial Responsibility:** A pay cut means a reduction in overall household income, at least temporarily. This may necessitate changes in lifestyle, spending habits, and financial planning. Having your spouse's understanding and co-operation in managing financial obligations, reducing unnecessary expenditures, and revising financial goals can make this transition much smoother.

3. **Perspective and Advice:** Your spouse, as an external observer, can offer a unique perspective or advice that you may not have considered. She knows your strengths, aspirations, and weaknesses, and her insights could be valuable when navigating the complexities of a career change.
4. **Motivation and Persistence:** The journey through a career change isn't typically a short one, and it isn't always smooth sailing. There will be moments of doubt, setbacks, and challenges. The role of a spouse as a cheerleader, reminding you of why you started this transition and encouraging you to persist, can be the much-needed motivation.
5. **Adapting to New Norms:** A career change may affect your daily routine, work hours, stress levels, or even your mood and demeanour. A supportive spouse can help you adapt to these new norms, providing patience, understanding, and flexibility as you navigate your new professional landscape.

Remember, in any significant life change, having a supportive partner can make the difference between a transition that feels insurmountable and one that feels like a shared adventure. It is a journey of growth, learning, and resilience, and having someone by your side, sharing the burden and cheering you on, is irreplaceable.

Money-related issues are one of the leading causes of stress in relationships and can lead to arguments and misunderstandings if not managed well. Money management as a couple is not just about numbers but also about understanding and respecting each other's values and priorities. Hence, effective communication and joint decision-making are the keys to managing money effectively as a couple.

Finance Insights:

What is the impact of marriage on family finances?

Marriage can significantly impact an individual's financial situation, and understanding these changes is crucial for maintaining financial health and planning for the future. Here are some ways in which marriage can affect family finances:

1. **Combined Incomes:** Perhaps the most immediate impact of marriage is the potential for a dual income. This can provide financial stability and increased purchasing power, but it also requires careful budgeting and decision-making to ensure that money is spent wisely.
2. **Shared Expenses:** Marriage often leads to shared financial responsibilities. Costs such as rent/mortgage, utilities, groceries, and other shared expenses can be divided, potentially lowering individual financial burdens.
3. **Tax Implications:** Depending on the couple's respective incomes, getting married can lead to tax benefits or liabilities. Some couples may fall into a higher tax bracket when their incomes are combined, known as the "marriage penalty." Others may receive a "marriage bonus" with lower tax liability due to income disparity between spouses.
4. **Insurance Policies:** After marriage, spouses can usually be added to health, auto, and home insurance policies. This can lead to lower rates through family or multi-driver policies. However, it is important to compare individual and combined policies to find the most cost-effective option.
5. **Retirement Planning:** Marriage often prompts couples to start or revise their retirement planning. Spouses can often contribute to each other's employer-sponsored retirement plans, and they may need to update beneficiaries on these accounts and other financial assets.
6. **Debt:** If one or both partners bring debt into the marriage, this can become a shared responsibility. This debt can impact the couple's overall financial health and decisions, including credit scores, loan approvals, and interest rates.
7. **Savings Goals:** Marriage usually means aligning and prioritising financial goals, such as buying a house, starting a family, or planning for vacations. This could require changes in savings and spending habits.
8. **Estate Planning:** Marriage typically necessitates updates to estate planning, including wills and inheritance. Spouses generally have legal rights to each other's estates, which can affect decisions about how property and assets are distributed in the event of death.

Thus, marriage is a significant financial partnership. It is important for couples to communicate openly about their finances, set shared goals, and make joint decisions about their income, expenses, savings, and investments.

With marriage, we both realised that life had changed; from being college-time sweethearts, we became responsible partners, and we both totally agreed with what Julie Andrews has said, "Marriage is like a graph—it has its ups and downs, and as long as things bounce back up again, you've got a good marriage. If it heads straight down, then you've got some problems!"

We both had many financial questions, like:

1. Can we upgrade our car?
2. When can we buy a new house? Would we buy it for investment, or should we move into the new home?
3. Should we live with our parents? Or should we move out?
4. Should my spouse take up a higher-pressure job, or should I take up one?
5. What finances should we disclose to and discuss with the family?
6. When should one plan to have a baby and start a family?
7. Are we financially independent and secure?

Managing finances as a couple requires a blend of effective communication, joint decision-making, respect for each other's values and priorities, and a comprehensive understanding of each other's financial habits. It is crucial to understand that each individual has a unique relationship with money – some are savers, some are spenders. Recognising your partner's financial persona will aid in constructing a well-rounded financial plan that respects these differences. Additionally, honesty plays a paramount role in managing finances as a couple. Be open about your financial history, including any past debts, loans, or financial obligations. This ensures the foundation of your shared financial future is rooted in trust and transparency.

Furthermore, fostering financial literacy as a couple can serve as a bonding experience and equip you with the tools to make informed financial decisions. There are numerous online resources available to help improve your understanding of budgeting, saving, and investing. Avoid keeping financial secrets, such as hidden purchases or debts, as they can lead to distrust and harm the relationship. Lastly, it is crucial to remember that every financial achievement, no matter how minor, deserves recognition. Celebrating these milestones can serve as motivation to continue working towards your financial goals. Overall, the ultimate objective of managing money as a couple is to ensure financial stability and security while aligning your financial practices and goals with your life objectives.

In conclusion, the importance of couples and money is a topic that deserves more attention, especially within educational institutions like colleges and universities. Integrating financial literacy discussions into the curriculum can help future generations build strong financial foundations and foster healthier relationships. However, achieving this cultural shift towards open financial communication and education requires collective efforts from society, institutions, and individuals. By recognizing the significance of managing money as a couple and embracing the principles of transparency, education, and celebration of financial milestones, we can pave the way for stronger, more secure, and more harmonious relationships built on a foundation of financial well-being.

"I am not a product of my circumstances. I am a product of my decisions."

– Stephen Covey

Chapter 5

"It's Not Just Child's Play": Unveiling the Financial Realities of Parenthood"

Diya and I decided against being a DINK (Dual Income No Kids) couple. In 2012, we were blessed with a daughter whom we named 'Krisha,' signifying 'Gift of God.' Given my family's devotion to Lord Krishna, the name 'Krisha' felt like an extension of that divine bond. In the fifth chapter, I will talk about the next aspect that shaped my journey – parenthood, and the unveiling of its profound financial realities, reshaping my understanding of wealth and investments.

As soon as Krisha arrived, everyone showered us with gifts, sweets, and an overwhelming amount of parenting advice. Questions about which school we'd chosen for her started pouring in. It felt like a tsunami of information, questions, tips, and tricks - too much for both of us to handle. Simultaneously, our mothers were advising us to start saving gold for our daughter's wedding. Diya and I were still coming to terms with the reality of being parents and learning the basics, like supporting Krisha's neck when holding her.

"Gold every month?" Diya looked at me with surprise. "I don't want gold! Take all the gold I have and instead give me experiences like scuba diving or bungee jumping."

I found myself pondering: would Krisha have similar preferences? Would she prefer wearing gold? But that's a conversation for another day.

The truth is, gold acts as an excellent buffer against inflation, serves as a safe haven during wartime, and most significantly, enjoys global acceptance. My mother wasn't wrong in suggesting that we incorporate gold into our investment portfolio. Gold isn't just valuable in an economic sense; it carries sentimental value, too. For instance, a necklace passed down from my grandmother to my mother and then, my wife, and potentially to Krisha, represents a cherished legacy.

Yet, gold wasn't the only consideration. My mother also talked about the need for a housemaid, a cook, and so much more. We had thought that our wedding was the most significant expenditure of our lives, but the birth of Krisha made us reconsider our ideas about money matters.

As an academician, I helped Diya put things into perspective. "You're not wrong," I told her, "Our wedding was the most significant one-time expense of our lives. But raising a child will be the largest recurring expense."

After some deliberation, we both agreed that "expense" might not be the right term. Raising a child is the most substantial recurring investment of our lives, with potentially infinite returns. After all, our parents invested in us throughout their lives; such is the ethos of our culture.

Finance Insights:

So, what is the impact of the birth of a child on a family's finances?

The birth of a child in a family is a joyous event, bringing with it significant financial implications, too. In fact, the financial implications begin much before the child is born, with maybe a baby shower or babymoon trip or a pregnancy photoshoot. Come on, don't we want to cherish these memories? Our reflections led us to list down the potential investments we'd be making in Krisha's journey:

1. **Early Education:** This was the foremost concern. Would we enrol her in a playschool or daycare before kindergarten? Many of our well-wishers recommended international preschools with their holistic approach to early childhood education, while others vouched for traditional methods.
2. **Primary and Secondary Education:** A good school in Mumbai can cost a fortune, and the fee hikes every year are daunting. And beyond

formal schooling, there are extracurricular classes – dance, music, and sports – each demanding its own set of expenses.

3. **Higher Education:** With college education becoming more specialised, we had to factor in tuition fees, living expenses, and other auxiliary costs. The rate at which education costs are rising, setting up a corpus for her higher education became paramount.
4. **Study Abroad:** The idea of Krisha wanting to study abroad wasn't too far-fetched. USA, UK, Australia, Canada – all popular destinations come with their exorbitant fees and living expenses.
5. **Travel and Exposure:** Diya and I believed that real education comes not just from books but from seeing the world. So, we wanted Krisha to travel, understand cultures, and broaden her horizons. This, too, would need a significant outlay.
6. **Medical Expenses:** Ensuring Krisha's health and well-being would always be a top priority. Regular medical check-ups, vaccinations, emergencies, dental care – all had to be budgeted for.
7. **Personal Development:** Hobbies, passion projects, and personal interests would need nurturing. Whether she wanted to learn the violin, take up horse riding, or attend a robotics workshop, we had to be prepared.
8. **Celebrations:** Birthday parties, graduation parties, and other significant milestones would bring their own share of expenses.
9. **General Living Expenses:** Clothing, food, transportation, and her personal gadgets or devices would all add up over the years.
10. **Savings:** With the arrival of a new family member, it is often necessary to revisit and adjust your savings strategy. This might include creating an emergency fund, saving for your child's education, or starting a retirement fund, if you haven't already done so.
11. **Insurance:** You may need to upgrade your health insurance to cover your child, and you may want to consider life insurance to protect your family's financial future in case something happens to you.
12. **Lower Income:** If one parent decides to leave work or reduce work hours to care for the child, this could lead to a reduction in family income.

As Diya and I sat down charting out these details, it was evident that planning for Krisha's future was no minor task. But, as parents, we were ready to give her the best we could, both materially and emotionally. However, we also acknowledged the importance of instilling values of humility, gratitude, and empathy in her, so that she could appreciate the privileges she would enjoy.

Raising Krisha would be the grandest adventure of our lives, filled with challenges, learning, joy, and of course, significant financial investments. But, as they say, the best things in life aren't 'things.' There are memories, experiences, and the legacy we leave behind. And for us, Krisha was the embodiment of all those priceless treasures.

As is clear by now, raising a child requires significant financial planning and resources. However, with careful budgeting, financial planning, and perhaps making some adjustments to lifestyle and spending habits, it is certainly manageable. It is recommended that families consider these factors and plan accordingly to ensure that they are financially prepared for the exciting journey of parenthood.

In conclusion, this chapter serves as a reminder that the decision to have a child is deeply personal, reflecting both individual desires and the fundamental human need for connection and family. Once you've made the choice to expand your family, it's essential to consider how many children you plan to have, as this decision carries both emotional and financial implications. It's crucial to recognize that this is a highly personal choice, one that should be made based on your unique circumstances and preferences rather than external pressures or societal norms.

As we've explored, the costs associated with raising a child can be substantial, both emotionally and financially. However, with thoughtful financial planning, budgeting, and lifestyle adjustments, these challenges can be navigated effectively. The key is to remain sensitive to your own needs and objectives as a couple, rather than succumbing to external influences.

Ultimately, the goal is to provide you with the tools to make informed decisions about your family's size and financial preparedness. By considering the variables and factors discussed in this chapter, you can choose what is best for you, both emotionally and financially, as you embark on the exciting journey of parenthood.

So managing the family finances after the birth of a child, indeed, is not child's play.

"Parenting is a life time job and does not stop when a child grows up."

–Jake Slope

Chapter 6

"Gyaan": Financial Literacy - After all I am a Teacher!

In today's rapidly evolving world, the significance of financial literacy cannot be understated. It is a vital life skill that enables individuals to navigate the complex terrains of money management, investments, savings, and more. But why is there a pressing need for enhancing financial education and awareness in our society today?

The profound statement made by the BJP MP, Tejasvi Surya, in December 2022, in Parliament encapsulates the essence of this urgency: "A large number of young Indians are entering the job market and the middle class for the first time. However, they are not equipped with essential money management skills, as financial literacy is not part of the country's formal school education system." Mr. Surya emphasises the necessity of integrating financial literacy into the school and college curriculum to safeguard young Indians from the pitfalls of poor financial decisions and the lures of dubious financial schemes.

In August 2023, Union Finance and Corporate Affairs Minister, Nirmala Sitharaman, also championed the cause during her address at a National CA Conference. She underscored the transformative power of technology in fostering financial literacy, especially in an era marked by the pervasive influence of digital platforms. During the trials of the COVID-19 Pandemic, many realised the potent strength of the digital world, and this revelation paved the way for more individuals, even those traditionally hesitant, to explore diverse financial avenues. Minister Sitharaman recognised and commended these efforts but was also quick to pinpoint the challenges. She stressed the need for more expansive financial literacy campaigns that resonate with India's linguistic diversity. The message was clear: to truly empower, financial literacy initiatives must be accessible and understandable to all.

Both these leaders have identified a critical gap in our educational framework and have highlighted the profound impact of equipping our youth with the tools of financial literacy. As we delve deeper into this chapter, we will explore the intricacies of financial literacy, the efforts of the regulators, MII's AMFI and AMCs, understanding its facets, and realising its potential to transform lives and fortify futures.

The efforts of regulators and financial bodies in advancing Investor Education and Awareness Initiatives (IEAI) are laudable. These endeavours, drawing on countless hours and the ingenuity of adept professionals, converge towards one vision: a financially savvy India. These initiatives are principally financed by mechanisms such as SEBI's (Investor Protection and Education Fund) Regulations, 2009, various Investor Protection Funds, and the Investor Education and Protection Fund (IEPF) pursuant to the Companies Act, 2013.

This chapter is penned with an intent to motivate active participation in these initiatives, which are, in essence, a product of our collective contributions—public funds aimed at public welfare. It is a call to action not only to engage but also to harness the power of social media to amplify the reach of these initiatives. After all, the true value of such investments of time, money, and resources is realized only when they touch the lives of those in need. Let us strive to ensure that these beneficial programs fulfil their potential by becoming accessible to every corner of our society.

Financial education and financial literacy are related but distinct concepts:

Financial Education

Financial education refers to the process of providing individuals with the knowledge, skills, and understanding necessary to make informed financial decisions. It involves formal or structured learning programmes, courses, or workshops that cover various aspects of personal finance, including budgeting, saving, investing, debt management, retirement planning, and more. Financial education aims to equip individuals with the knowledge and tools they need to navigate the complexities of the financial world effectively. It is usually delivered by educators, financial institutions, government agencies, or non-profit organisations.

Financial education also supports the achievement of Sustainable Development Goal (SDG) - No. 4 on Education, which aims to ensure inclusive and equitable quality education and promote lifelong learning opportunities for all (SDG Target 4.6 on Literacy and SDG Target 4.4 on Life Skills under SDG 4 on Education).

Financial Literacy

Financial literacy, on the other hand, is the practical application of the financial knowledge and skills gained through financial education. It is the ability of individuals to understand and apply financial concepts to manage their personal finances effectively. Financial literacy encompasses the capability to budget, save, invest, borrow responsibly, and make informed financial decisions based on one's financial knowledge. It is the measure of an individual's financial competence in handling everyday financial matters.

In essence, financial education is the process of learning and acquiring financial knowledge, while financial literacy is the outcome of that learning – the ability to use that knowledge to make sound financial decisions in real-life situations. Financial education lays the foundation for financial literacy, enabling individuals to confidently manage their finances and achieve their financial goals. Both financial education and financial literacy are essential components of promoting financial well-being and empowering individuals to take charge of their financial futures.

The Organisation for Economic Co-operation and Development (OECD, 2008) defines financial literacy as "Knowledge and understanding of financial concepts, and the skills, motivation, and confidence to apply such knowledge and understanding in order to make effective decisions across a range of financial contexts, to improve the financial well-being of individuals and society, and to enable participation in economic life." The OECD INFE (2012) has defined financial literacy as follows: "A combination of awareness, knowledge, skill, attitude, and behaviour necessary to make sound financial decisions and ultimately achieve individual financial well-being."

The OECD INFE definition is the most widely accepted definition of financial literacy.

Investor awareness is the term used in the investor community to describe the level of knowledge of investors about the investment environment, which includes their investment rights and obligations, laws and procedures, types of investments, investment service providers, and their control mechanisms, among other things.

The level of awareness helps measure or benchmark the investor's exposure and knowledge about the information in the industry as a whole. The significance of awareness is that investors are expected to base their investment decisions on market information. In the absence of access to market information, the investor may have a lower profile among their peers in the market. Thus, investor awareness contributes directly or indirectly to the competitive advantage of business participants in identifying potential investment opportunities, which ultimately leads to the achievement of investment objectives.

Why is Financial Literacy Important?

As India completes its 75th year of independence, achieving financial freedom is crucial for the nation's holistic development, and financial literacy is the only way to achieve financial freedom.

Financial freedom is essential as it lays the foundation for individuals to take control of their economic fate, make informed decisions, and become less dependent on external circumstances for their financial well-being. It allows individuals to make choices that can lead to a more fulfilled life, such as pursuing passions, starting businesses, or early retirement. Additionally, financial freedom implies the availability of a safety net in the event of financial downturns or personal emergencies. This level of security reduces stress and provides peace of mind, ultimately leading to improved mental health and a better quality of life. On a broader scale, a financially independent population is the key to driving economic growth, reducing societal inequalities, and fostering resilience against economic shocks. If India is financially literate, it can be financially resilient and achieve economic growth.

To understand why financial literacy is so important, let us review some of the studies conducted on the topic:

The Standard & Poor's Financial Services LLC (S&P), FinLit Survey 2015 findings are sobering. Worldwide, only 1-in-3 adults are financially literate. The S&P Global FinLit Survey is the largest, most comprehensive measure of financial literacy. The survey provides key information to policy makers, regulators, the private sector, and academics, empowering them to develop effective financial education policies and programmes.

According to the survey, less than 25% of adults are financially literate in South Asian countries. For the average Indian, financial literacy has yet to become a priority. India is home to 17.5% of the world's population, but nearly 76% of its adult population cannot understand basic financial concepts. These results are glaring and require immediate intervention to increase the financial literacy Level in the Country.

Financial ignorance carries significant costs. Consumers who fail to understand the concept of interest compounding spend more on transaction fees, run up bigger debts, and incur higher interest rates on loans (Lusardi and Tufano, 2015; Lusardi and de Bassa Scheresberg, 2013). They also end up borrowing more and saving less money (Stango and Zinman, 2009). Meanwhile, the potential benefits of financial literacy are manifold. People with strong financial skills do a better job planning and saving for retirement (Behrman et al., 2012; Lusardi and Mitchell, 2014). Financially savvy investors are more likely to diversify risk by spreading funds across several ventures (Abreu and Mendes, 2010).

The NCFE – All India Financial Inclusion and Financial Literacy Survey in 2019 confirmed the S&P FinLit Survey report. This survey revealed that 27.18% of the respondents have achieved the minimum target score in each of the components of financial literacy prescribed by OECD INFE. This means that approximately 73% of the respondents in India could not achieve the correct score, revealing low levels of Financial Literacy in India.

The COVID-19 Pandemic has been an unprecedented crisis and has not only impacted our health but also our education, wealth, and the economy as a whole. Price Waterhouse Coopers (PWC) – 10th Annual – Employee Wellness Survey, 2021 revealed some thought-provoking results. After a year of disruption in people's lives due to COVID-19, finances are the top cause of employee stress, even above job, health, and relationship stress combined. 63% of employees say that their financial stress has increased since the start of the pandemic.

This phenomenon is validated by the Employees Provident Fund Organisation (EPFO), which allowed formal sector workers under its ambit to withdraw a non-refundable advance from their retirement savings to deal with hardships due to the lockdown. 8.2 lakh workers decided to dip into their PF savings to survive during the COVID-19 lockdown, which shows the deplorable financial condition of the workers. EPFO settled 56.79 lakh COVID-19 advance claims and released over ₹14,000 crores till December 2020, demonstrating the tremendous impact on the financial well-being of the workers.

The PWC Employee Wellness Survey 2019 studied a very interesting correlation between the degree of care the employer has about the financial well-being of an employee and their loyalty towards the organisation. Forty-six percent of millennials and 44 percent of members of Generation X (compared with 30 percent of Baby Boomers) polled in the survey said loyalty to their employer was influenced by how much the company cared about their financial well-being. The majority in all three age groups (81% of millennials, 75% of Generation X, and 52% of Baby Boomers) said another company that cared more about their financial well-being would be more attractive to them.

The studies cited above conclude that India has come a long way, with literacy levels having improved considerably from a mere 18.3% in 1951 to 74.4% in 2018. However, the financial literacy rates have been a concern. So, there is an increased need in the 75th year of India's Independence to provide for the knowledge, skills, and attitude of managing one's money, which will help people achieve financial well-being.

In view of achieving financial well-being, The National Centre for Financial Education (NCFE), in consultation with the four Financial Sector Regulators and other relevant stakeholders, has developed the

National Strategy for Financial Education 2020-2025. This strategy was approved by TGFIFL and FSDC, Ministry of Finance, Government of India.

The National Strategy for Financial Education (NSFE) is defined as "a nationally coordinated approach to financial education that consists of an adapted framework or programme" (OECD, 2019). The NSFE document intends to support the vision of the Government of India and Financial Sector Regulators by enabling various sections of the population to develop knowledge, skills, attitudes, and behaviours needed to manage their money better and plan for their future. The document also takes stock of the current work done by various stakeholders and adopts a multi-stakeholder approach to achieve the financial well-being of Indians.

It is envisaged that implementing the Strategy would go a long way in furthering financial literacy across the country and result in positive behavioural outcomes among the population emanating from the Strategic Objectives laid down in the document.

To achieve the Strategic Objectives laid down by the new NSFE, it has been recommended to adopt the 5-Core Actions / 5-C Approach through the emphasis on the development of relevant content, developing capacity of the various intermediaries involved in providing financial services, leveraging the facilitating role of a community-led model for financial literacy through an appropriate communication strategy by enhancing collaboration among various stakeholders.

Financial literacy and financial education have garnered the attention of all stakeholders. Commendable efforts have been made by all regulators in this domain. I have had the privilege of meeting officers, General Managers, and Chief General Managers from many regulatory bodies, and I must commend their significant contribution to financial literacy and investor education. Below are some of the initiatives undertaken by these regulators to promote financial literacy.

Financial Literacy/ Financial Education initiatives by various Financial Regulators and Bodies

As suggested earlier let us dwell deeper into the efforts of regulators and financial institutions towards creating a financially literate India.

I. RBI's Initiatives on Financial Education

Financial Inclusion and Education are two important elements in the Reserve Bank of India's developmental role. Towards this, it has created a comprehensive volume of literature and has uploaded it on its website in 13 languages, which banks and other stakeholders can download and use. The aim of this initiative is to create awareness about financial products and services, good financial practices, going digital, and consumer protection.

1. **Financial Awareness Message (FAME)**

   In a move to provide elementary financial literacy information to the general public, RBI has designed the booklet FAME (Financial Awareness Messages). FAME contains financial awareness messages, such as documents needed to be submitted while opening a bank account (KYC), the importance of budgeting, saving, and responsible borrowing, maintaining creditworthiness, a credit score and repaying loans on time, doorstep banking, and localised banking, the process of lodging complaints at the bank and the Banking Ombudsman, usage of electronic transfers, capitalising money in registered entities, etc. Audio-visuals have also been produced to create awareness on topics like "Basic Financial Literacy," "Unified Payments Interface," and "Going Digital." The pictorial booklet series of Reserve Bank named 'Raju and Money Kumar' is also effective. The booklet 'Raju' teaches about banking concepts and savings habits, and 'Money Kumar' clarifies the role and functions of the Reserve Bank of India.

2. **Be(A)ware & Raju and the Forty Thieves**

   As part of the Reserve Bank of India's customer awareness initiatives, the office released a booklet titled 'Be(A)ware' in July 2021, which highlights the methods employed by financial fraudsters. Encouraged by the positive feedback from the public and various institutions, the RBI is advancing its commitment to financial education. The aim is to make this information more accessible to those new to the digital financial realm, especially those unfamiliar with the intricacies of online financial transactions. This target group encompasses individuals of various age groups and educational backgrounds, including school children, young adults, semi-literate individuals, and senior citizens, regardless of their location—whether it's urban, rural, or semi-urban areas. The booklet is designed to raise awareness among those who are just stepping into the digital domain, emphasising the fundamentals of digital financial transactions.

Titled 'Raju and the Forty Thieves,' the booklet comprises 40 stories that shed light on the fraudulent activities reported to the RBI. These stories also provide straightforward advice on the Do's and Don'ts of online transactions. In these tales, Raju, depicted as a naive citizen, is portrayed in various roles—sometimes as a senior citizen, sometimes as a farmer, and other times as a carefree individual. However, his distinctive curly hair remains consistent, symbolising that people from all walks of life can always relate to him. It's essential for everyone to educate themselves about the tactics used by these fraudsters and to ensure that those around them are also well-informed and vigilant against such financial scams.

3. **Financial Literacy Week**

   The Financial Literacy Week is an initiative by RBI to promote awareness on key topics every year through a focused campaign. Financial Literacy Week 2023 was observed from February 13-17, 2023, on the theme of "Good Financial Behaviour - Your Saviour." The messages disseminated during the week focused on Savings, planning, and budgeting.

4. **"Project Financial Literacy."**

   The objective of this project is to disseminate information regarding the central bank and general banking concepts to various target groups, including school and college students, women, rural and urban poor, defence personnel, and senior citizens. The project envisages a multi-pronged approach. The project has been designed to be implemented in two modules, one module focusing on the economy, RBI, and its activities, and the other module on general banking. The material is created in English and other vernacular languages. It is disseminated to the target audience with the help of banks, local government machinery, schools, and colleges through presentations, pamphlets, brochures, films, and also through RBI's website.

In addition to the above, RBI has also undertaken the following initiatives:

Important press releases, statements, regulatory guidelines, speeches, clarifications, and events are tweeted on RBI's Twitter handle '@RBI,' and videos are relayed on RBI's YouTube link. A separate Twitter handle '@RBI says' and Facebook page 'RBI Says' publish messages and information of interest for greater awareness and understanding of the Bank's functions. Reserve Bank of India envisages limited two-way communication and engagement over social media and monitors its social media presence.

Over the years, RBI has been constantly reaching out to the common man through outreach programmes, financial literacy initiatives, mass media, social media platforms, etc. Reserve Bank of India also empowers the public by informing them about facilities and services to expect from banks and financial institutions through Public Awareness Campaigns, which aim at educating them regarding their rights and responsibilities in banking-related matters. The campaigns are done on a regular basis in newspapers, TV, radio, cinema, digital channels, SMS, and hoardings, under the tagline 'RBI Kehta Hai.'

A film on BSBDAs explains how opening this account obviates the requirement of a minimum balance. A film on 'Safe Digital Banking' cautions the public about sharing card and PIN details while carrying out digital transactions. Another film on 'Limited Liability' explains the recourse available in the event of card fraud. A film on 'Ease of Banking for Senior Citizens' elucidates facilities like doorstep banking available for senior citizens. These films, using cricketers and badminton players who are employees of the Reserve Bank of India, were widely disseminated in media advertisements.

A unique feature of the public awareness campaign is the missed call element: upon giving a missed call to the number 14440, the caller will receive information through a pre-recorded Interactive Voice Response System (IVRS), avoiding the miscommunication or over-communication of a Call Centre approach. In the non-Hindi-speaking regions, mobile phone subscribers receive messages in English and regional languages, so that the connection with the common person is immediate and all-encompassing.

II. Securities and Exchange Board of India

The Preamble of the Securities and Exchange Board of India describes the basic functions of the Securities and Exchange Board of India as "...to protect the interests of investors in securities and to promote the development of, and to regulate the securities market and for matters connected therewith or incidental thereto."

The regulator, as per the preamble of the act, has undertaken many measures to impart financial education and investor awareness among the various target groups. These measures have been recognized internationally in the IOSCO report and other international organizations, which shows the commendable work done in this space.

Some of the initiatives of SEBI towards investor education and awareness are as follows:

1. **Basic Financial Education:**

   SEBI has the following initiatives for basic financial education:

   a. **Financial Education through Resource Persons Programme to impart financial education to the public:**

      Eligible individuals trained and impanelled as RPs (in districts) by SEBI can conduct free workshops in the local language and are paid an honorarium. The basic concepts of finance, banking, insurance, pension, and investments are covered across five target groups (viz. Home Makers, Self-Help groups, Executives, Middle-Income Groups, and Retired personnel). During the workshops, free financial education booklets are distributed.

   b. Visit to SEBI by students

   c. Financial Education Booklet covering basics of concepts like Financial planning, Savings, Investment, Insurance, Pension, Borrowing, Tax saving, caution against Ponzi schemes, Grievance redressal, etc.

2. **Sector-Specific Financial Education:**

   SEBI has the following initiatives for sector-focused financial education:

   a. Investor awareness programmes by SEBI-recognised Investors' Associations.

b. Regional Seminars in association with Exchanges/Depositories.

c. Commodity awareness programmes by SEBI-recognised Commodity Derivatives Trainers.

3. **Investor Charter:** The investor charter proposed in Union Budget 2021-2022 with the aim of protecting investors from the mis-selling of financial products was cleared for launch by SEBI in its Board meeting on September 28, 2021. SEBI has framed the Investor Charter to promote transparency and enhance awareness, trust, and confidence among the investors. The Investor Charter, inter alia, includes the vision and mission statement, rights and responsibilities of investors, investor grievance redressal mechanism, and Dos and Don'ts for investing in the securities market. The Investor Charter also gives a broader perspective on the various rights and responsibilities of investors.

SEBI has also issued guidelines on Investor Charters to the following entities and advised them to develop their own investor charters on the lines of the broad guidelines provided by SEBI. This charter is a brief document describing different services to investors at a single place for ease of reference.

SEBI, via various circulars, has instructed Publishing Investor Charter and Disclosure of Investor Complaints by the following institutions:

1. Stock Exchanges
2. Depositories
3. Merchant Bankers on their Websites for private placement of units by InvITs proposed to be listed
4. Registrar and Transfer Agents (RTAs)
5. Mutual Funds and AMFI
6. Investment advisers on their website and mobile applications
7. Research Analysts on their website and mobile application
8. Custodians and Designated Depository Participants (DDPs)
9. Portfolio Managers
10. Alternate Investment Funds
11. Debenture Trustees

In addition to the above-mentioned institutions, SEBI has also undertaken the following initiatives.

1. **Participation in the World Investor Week in association with the International Organization of Securities Commissions (IOSCO):** With the objective of highlighting the initiatives undertaken by various financial market regulators in the direction of conducting investor protection and education awareness activities, IOSCO has been organizing a week-long global campaign every year referred to as World Investor Week (WIW). SEBI participated in IOSCO WIW by organising various financial literacy and investor awareness programmes during this week across the country. This year, SEBI has informed the participants that the WIW will be celebrated from the 9th to the 15th of October 2023, and the theme of this year's WIW is 'Investors Resilience'. A few ways in which we can build resilience amongst investors whom we speak to are:
   a. Be prepared with an emergency fund.
   b. Ensure that your portfolio is diversified.
   c. Don't expose yourself to potential investment losses you cannot afford.
   d. Do your research before investing.
   e. And, last but not least, watch out for investment fraud.
2. **Dedicated Investor Website:** A dedicated website http://investor.sebi.gov.in is maintained for the benefit of investors. The website provides relevant educational/ awareness material and other useful information. Further, schedules of various investor and financial education programmes are also displayed on the website for the information of investors.
3. **Mass Media Campaign:** In order to reach out to people, SEBI has embarked on a mass media campaign, giving relevant messages to investors through popular media. Since 2012, SEBI has carried out various awareness campaigns in multi-mass media (TV/Radio/Print/bulk SMS) on the topics mentioned below:
   - Investor grievance redressal mechanism
   - Collective Investment Scheme - Unrealistic returns.

- Collective Investment Scheme – Don't Go by Hearsay.
- Application Supported by Blocked Amount (ASBA) - Initial Public Offering (IPO). Dabba Trading.
- Caution against Hot Tips.

Additionally, posters on cautionary messages listed above were printed in various languages and distributed to district collectors, panchayat offices, etc., in various languages.

4. **Investor Grievance Redressal:** SEBI has been taking various regulatory measures to expedite the redressal of investor grievances. The grievances lodged by investors are taken up with the respective listed company or intermediary and continuously monitored. SEBI Complaints Redressal System (SCORES) has helped the investors in real-time knowledge of the status of their grievances since investors can log onto SCORES at any time and from anywhere and check the status of the grievances with the help of the username and password provided to them at the time of lodging grievances.
5. **SEBI Toll-Free Helpline:** SEBI launched a toll-free helpline service with numbers 1800 22 7575/1800 266 7575 on December 30, 2011. The helpline service is available every day from 9:00 a.m. to 6:00 p.m. (except on declared public holidays in Maharashtra) to investors from all over India. The helpline service is available in English, Hindi, and various regional languages.

III. Insurance Regulatory and Development Authority of India (IRDAI)

Since its inception, IRDAI has undertaken various initiatives in the area of financial literacy. Awareness programmes have been conducted on television and radio, and simple messages about the rights and duties of policyholders, channels available for dispute redressal, etc., have been disseminated through television, radio, and print media, through sustained campaigns in English, Hindi, and 11 other Indian languages.

IRDAI has conducted a pan-India survey on awareness levels about insurance, carried out through the NCAER, in a bid to improve its strategy of creating insurance awareness. A post-launch survey was also carried out to gauge the efficacy of the campaigns of IRDAI in increasing insurance penetration and awareness. IRDAI has also brought out publications of 'Policyholder Handbooks' as well as a comic book series on insurance. A dedicated website for consumer education in insurance was launched to reach out to the policyholders more effectively. IRDAI's Integrated Grievance Management System (IGMS) creates a central repository of grievances across the country and provides for various analyses of data indicative of areas of concern to the insurance policyholder.

Some of the major initiatives carried out by IRDAI are listed below:

1. Conducting seminars, awareness campaigns, Metro Rail campaigns, quizzes, etc.
2. "Young Corner" - an interactive six-game feature was launched on the Policyholders website. A Hindi version of the website was also launched to increase its reach.
3. A Print campaign cautioning the general public about the spurious callers and fictitious offers was launched. Insurance comic books in 12 vernacular languages were released.
4. Handbooks on Insurance, such as Employment opportunities in Insurance for students.
5. Crop Insurance, right buying, etc., were launched.
6. A pan-India campaign against spurious callers through TV Commercials and Radio jingles on the utility and benefits of various forms of insurance in five regional languages.

IV. Pension Fund Regulatory Development Authority (PFRDA)

1. PFRDA launched a dedicated website called 'Pension Sanchay' in 2018. Through this website, PFRDA aims to address the need for financial literacy from the perspective of retirement planning. The content of the website has been designed keeping in mind the four most important concepts in financial decision-making: knowledge of interest rates, interest compounding, inflation, and risk diversification. The website has a separate blog segment where blogs written by professionals and authorities in the financial sector are made available, providing meaningful insights regarding the fundamentals of finance, banking, and investments.

2. PFRDA conducts subscriber awareness programmes through its central record-keeping agencies at different places across India. Further, PFRDA has also empaneled a dedicated training agency for creating subscriber awareness and capacity-building regarding the NPS and APY. In addition to the above, PFRDA also conducts the Annuity Literacy Programme in coordination with NPS Trust and Annuity Service Providers to make subscribers aware of the different annuities available to them.

V. National Bank for Agriculture and Rural Development (NABARD)

1. Creation of financial awareness among rural masses through various media in Hindi, English, and vernacular languages: Printed materials such as leaflets, posters, books/booklets on financial literacy initiatives; jingles related to financial inclusion, e.g., opening of bank accounts, SHG savings, Swarojgar Credit Cards, etc., were aired, and animated films on loans, budgeting, and the usage of ATMs. hosted on the NABARD website as well as the YouTube channel.
2. Conduct of Financial Literacy Awareness Programmes (FLAPs) targeted for people who are newly inducted into the financial system - adults, farmers, school children, senior citizens, SHGs, and entrepreneurs, besides financial education for rural masses on different modes of digital payments.
3. Conduct of FLAPs with Mobile Demo Vans fitted with Audio-Video equipment, ATM, Micro ATM, and handholding for conducting digital transactions.
4. Capacity-building initiatives to sensitise and train the staff of commercial banks, RRBs, and RCBs for effective delivery of financial literacy through BIRD. Setting up financial literacy centres by Regional Rural Banks (RRBs) and Rural Cooperative Banks (RCBs) besides deployment of mobile demonstration vans fitted with ATMs. and/or Micro-ATMs. 7) Extended support to Rural Self-Employment Training Institutes (RSETIs) / Rural Development & Self-Employment Training Institute (RUDSETI) to acquire training equipment for livelihood training.

5. Capacity-building initiatives to sensitise and train the staff of commercial banks, RRBs, and RCBs for effective delivery of financial literacy.
6. Training for BC/BFs of banks and reimbursement of examination fees.
7. NABARD has advised banks (scheduled commercial banks, RCBs, RRBs) to draw up state-wise quarterly plans for support from FIF towards financial and digital literacy camps by their branches and FLCs. These plans would have to cover target groups such as SHGs, students, senior citizens, farmers, small entrepreneurs, etc., giving special attention to excluded blocks, areas based on FIPs of Banks, and discussions in SLBC Sub Committee on FI and State Government priorities. NABARD RO would also be holding quarterly reviews with banks for projects funded out of FIF, and the progress would also be reviewed in the FI Sub Committee of SLBCs.

VI. SIDBI

1. *Samriddhi*, the virtual assistant, was launched by SIDBI on the Udyami Mitra portal on April 2, 2018. The virtual assistant guides budding entrepreneurs across a wide gamut of topics, ranging from kinds of loans to handholding support (operational in English and Hindi).
2. A "Bankability Kit for MSE Entrepreneurs" in bilingual format has been hosted on the portal. This is a one-stop guide for entrepreneurs to assess themselves, give an overview of what bankers look at, tips to communicate with banks, and financial products for MSMEs, among other important components.
3. Certified Credit Counsellors and CCIs have been empaneled on the Udyami Mitra platform to strengthen the supply side by enhancing access to credit and also giving thrust to the demand side issues of MSMEs, particularly those at the bottom of the pyramid.
4. The Udyami Mitra Portal aims at instilling ease of access to MSMEs' financial and non-financial service needs. The portal also hosts 325 project profiles, covering 40 industrial sectors for reference purposes. More than 7,618 handholding agencies have attended to 50,680

information and other important needs of aspirant entrepreneurs. Certified Credit Counsellors are also assisting entrepreneurs in enhancing their knowledge and connecting them appropriately with lenders.

5. SIDBI, with the support of the nationwide Common Service Centres (CSCs), has delivered an Entrepreneurship Awareness campaign for the Udyam Abhilasha project, which focused on 115 aspirational districts across 28 states. These 115 districts account for more than 20% of the country's population and cover over 8,600 *Gram Panchayats*. During the campaign, around 470 training locations were covered with over 2.25 lakh hours of inputs given to 18,000+ youths (including about 35% women).
6. SIDBI has positioned Hauz Khas Metro Station (in New Delhi) as a thematic station for disseminating information amongst the masses. This initiative aims at connecting people with initiatives like *Pradhan Mantri Mudra Yojana*, CGTMSE, Social Security schemes, SIDBI offerings, GOI initiatives, etc.
7. During the recent *Kumbh Mela*, SIDBI initiated a special project by setting up a *Swavalamban* stall and created financial awareness, aimed at spreading entrepreneurship culture across the nation, through games (*Kaun Banega Udyami*), Nukkad Natak/puppet shows, and financial literacy videos and disseminated information on schemes such as MUDRA, CGTMSE, Stand-Up India, and so on.

VII. National Payment Corporation of India (NPCI)

1. NPCI started working with Public Sector Banks (PSUs) and private sector banks to create awareness and literacy sessions on RuPay, IMPS, AePS, and USSD - *99#. NPCI was involved with cooperative and regional rural banks. While conducting awareness and literacy sessions, NPCI also distributed posters, ATM screens, web banners, SMS, emailers, etc., for digital payment literacy and fraud awareness.
2. Disseminating digital payment literacy to corporate employees and beneficiaries with the help of these agencies. Currently, apart from the banks, NCPL is associated with Indian Railways, OMCs, NABARD, Education Institutes, Corporate CSR, NULM, MFIs, BCs, NGOs,

Agritechs, FinTechs, etc., to promote digital payment literacy and awareness.

3. NCPL entered the Limca Book of Records in the year 2017 for conducting 120 e-payment literacy camps, simultaneously, across the country on September 8, 2015, the World Literacy Day. 23,930 customers attended workshops organised by NCPL.

VIII. Bombay Stock Exchange (BSE Ltd)

1. The BSE, through its Investor Protection Fund (IPF), regularly conducts Investor Awareness Programmes (IAPs) throughout the country. IPF was instrumental in organising 12,398 IAPs during FY 2022-23. Out of this, 4,926 IAPs were conducted through the IPF while 7,472 IAPs were conducted through the Investors Services Fund (ISF). During the year, IPF conducted 190 Regional Investor Seminars jointly with SEBI across different parts of the country. IPF also periodically publishes TV, print, digital, and online advertisements regarding Do's and Don'ts for investors, in order to educate them and enable them to safeguard their interests. During the year, several educational and other capital market awareness events were sponsored by IPF to raise awareness about corporate best practices. During the year, IPF has managed 27 Investor Service Centres across India, covering all the major state capitals, including Mumbai.
2. **World Investor Week (WIW) 2022:** BSE IPF celebrated the globally popular event for investors called World Investor Week (WIW 2022) under the aegis of SEBI and the International Organisation of Securities Commissions (IOSCO), from October 10-16, 2022. WIW is a week-long global celebration, promoted by the IOSCO to raise awareness about the importance of investor education and protection. In India, SEBI worked with all the Market Infrastructure Institutions to make this a memorable and enriching week for all investors. To mark the beginning of WIW celebrations, a bell-ringing ceremony was held on October 10, 2022, in BSE's International Convention Hall with Shri G P Garg, Executive Director, SEBI, as the Chief Guest, Shri Neeraj Kulshrestha, Chief Regulatory Officer, BSE along with Shri Bhavesh Vora, IPF Trustee and several senior dignitaries from SEBI and leading investor associations. During the said Bell-Ringing

Ceremony, the following key activities were undertaken by BSE IPF to celebrate WIW 2022.

a. **Launch of Financial Housie game called "FINHOUSIE":** It was an interesting fun-and-learn activity conducted during WIW. It served as a learning and gamification tool used for investor education and awareness, allowing participants to test their knowledge about the securities market in a fun and engaging manner.

b. **Investors Awareness Programmes (IAPs):** To spread knowledge and education about investing in the securities market by observing the qualities of a prudent investor, BSE IPF organised a total of 1,168 IAPs during WIW 2022, including 8 IAPs conducted jointly with SEBI and CDSL, 22 IAPs in partnership with CDSL, and the remaining 1,138 were conducted by various resource persons affiliated with BSE IPF/ISF. The total number of investors reached through these programmes was 67,424.

c. **Quiz Programmes:** A series of Quiz programmes were held on each day of WIW 2022 as follows:

   i. For the first 5 days, an Online Nationwide Investor Quiz on capital markets was conducted free of cost, with 3,219 contestants participating. A Referral Guidebook was provided to all the registered participants to educate them about various aspects of the securities market and help them prepare for the Quiz. The Quiz was conducted every day from 3:00 pm to 6:00 pm. The top 10 winners were selected each day and awarded gift vouchers. Furthermore, the top two winners from all five days received a special Certificate and a gift voucher.

   ii. Special Quiz Programme on Commodity Derivatives Segment: To spread awareness about Commodity Derivatives, as advised by SEBI, a Quiz programme was conducted exclusively on questions based on the Commodity Derivatives Segment. A set of Multiple-Choice Questions provided by SEBI was sent to all the registered participants, with 2,039 contestants participating in the quiz. The top 10 winners were awarded gift vouchers.

iii. National-level Quiz for students of the Institute of Company Secretaries of India (ICSI): Recognising the importance of governance and enhancing knowledge related to the governance framework applicable to listed entities, a nationwide Quiz was conducted for the students of ICSI, in collaboration with ICSI, wherein 2,146 students registered, and 943 participated. The top 10 winners were awarded gift vouchers.

VIII. National Stock Exchange

The National Stock Exchange of India (NSE) is deeply invested in fostering financial literacy, recognizing its pivotal role in the growth and stability of the securities market. The NSE's investor education initiatives are diverse and extensive, encompassing:

1. **Leveraging Media:** NSE disseminates targeted messages through SMS, emails, radio, newspapers, and social media in multiple languages to spread financial literacy and caution investors to make informed decisions.
2. **Webinars and Awareness Programs:** Over 3,800 programs were conducted across the country, utilizing digital platforms to educate investors of all backgrounds, especially during the pandemic.
3. **Initiatives for Entrepreneurs and Health Workers:** The NSE launched the 'Nurture Your Prosperity' initiative for startups and conducted focused sessions for health workers, acknowledging their service during COVID-19. They also organized workshops and discussions on Sustainable Finance and ESG.
4. **World Investor Week Participation:** NSE participates in this global campaign to highlight the importance of investor education and protection, aligning with SEBI's key messages and promoting financial literacy through various media. A vital part of this commitment is the participation in the World Investor Week 2023, which is a global campaign led by SEBI and IOSCO to promote investor education and protection. During this event, the NSE conducted a variety of activities, including informative sessions in regional languages, panel discussions, engaging financial quizzes, podcast series by experts, and

street plays known as 'nukkad natak'. These initiatives are designed to provide insights into investment opportunities, encourage safe and responsible investing habits, and educate on the dos and don'ts of investing.

5. **Tier II and Tier III Cities:** The NSE endeavours to reach a broad audience through digital, visual, and physical mediums, including creative approaches like puppetry and folk-dance performances to convey essential investment messages in tier II and tier III cities.

The NSE's endeavours demonstrate a commitment to empowering investors, ensuring they have the knowledge and skills for safe investment practices and long-term financial well-being.

IX. Central Depository Services Limited (CDSL)

CDSL empowers investors by educating them about Depository, capital market Practices, and the Rights and Obligations of the Investor. To this end, CDSL regularly conducts Investor Awareness Programmes (IAPs) in collaboration with the regulator, SEBI, its DPs, Exchanges, Financial / Educational Institutions, and other stakeholders.

CDSL Investor Protection Fund (CDSL IPF) conducts various investor awareness activities aimed at promoting financial education from the Depository point of view and other capital market initiatives in general. The goal is to educate investors to make informed decisions regarding any matter related to the capital market and become Atmanirbhar Niveshak, or self-sufficient investors.

CDSL IPF continually conducts Investor Awareness Programmes (IAPs) in association with SEBI, Market Infrastructure Institutions (MIIs), Financial Institutions, Professional Entities, Mutual Funds, Colleges and universities, Government Officials, Corporate Employees, etc., primarily targeting retail and potential investors. CDSL believes that investor education can significantly contribute to achieving financial inclusion in the capital market. During FY 2022-23, CDSL IPF conducted 1,552 IAPs in English, Hindi, and 16 other languages across India, using both online and offline modes, reaching over 1 Lakh investors across India, including Tier 2, Tier 3, and Tier 4 Towns/Cities.

To enhance financial education on a broader scale, CDSL has also engaged with investors through various social media platforms like Facebook (@cdslindia), Twitter (@cdslindia), LinkedIn (@cdslindia), KOO App (@cdslindia), Instagram (@cdslindia), and YouTube (@cdslindiaLtd). Various posts, including pictures, GIFs, and videos related to IAPs, along with awareness information about various services provided by CDSL, are shared for the benefit of investors.

CDSL also provides valuable information for investors on its website under the heading 'Investors Corner.' An informative booklet on "Securities Market Understanding from an Investor's Perspective," prepared jointly by SEBI, CDSL, and other MIIs in 13 regional languages (English, Malayalam, Punjabi, Hindi, Marathi, Gujarati, Telugu, Tamil, Oriya, Kannada, Assamese, Manipuri, Bengali) has been uploaded on the CDSL website at https://www.cdslindia.com/Investors/InvestorCorner.aspx. This booklet is shared with investors during IAPs to support their knowledge-building and future reference.

25 Years Celebration of CDSL

In 2023, CDSL embarks on its 25th year with the indomitable concept of 'Empowering Atmanirbharta,' with the nexus of human-tech forms at the very core of their endeavour to empower the Indian capital markets. As part of its 25th-anniversary celebrations, CDSL has undertaken the following initiatives:

CDSL Neev: CDSL Neev is a pan-India campaign aimed at spreading financial literacy and creating awareness about the opportunities presented by the capital markets. These sessions equip individuals from diverse backgrounds with a deeper understanding of the Indian capital markets and wealth management, empowering them to take control of their financial futures and make sound investment decisions.

X. National Securities Depository Limited (NSDL): NSDL strives to help the investor community by enabling it to become 'Prudent Investors.' NSDL organises Investor Awareness programmes for various segments of investors, including retail investors, corporate employees, college faculty and staff, students, the Indian Army, the Indian Navy, Police officials,

Railway officials, Prison officers, and senior citizens across India. The programmes are conducted in various languages and cover a variety of investor-related topics.

During the Year 2022-2023, NSDL has conducted 1088 IAPs and touched the lives of 97,000-plus beneficiaries. Among the unique programmes conducted by NSDL was an IAP at 5,600 ft above sea level at Anantnag, Jammu & Kashmir, and an AP for Prison Officers of Daulatrao Jadhav Yerawada Jail, Pune, Maharashtra.

Focused Programmes for Defence Personnel: NSDL believed in "Serving those who serve the Nation." In 2022–23, NSDL has conducted special programmes for Defence personnel serving in the Indian Army and the Indian Navy, along with the Border Security Force (BSF) jawans. These sessions discussed the importance of investing in Capital Markets, covering the basic concepts like the power of compounding, savings, and investments, and the different investment avenues available.

Programmes in Association with Other Market Participants: NSDL conducts awareness programmes in association with Depository Participants, SEBI, Stock Exchanges, and other corporations involved in capital markets. These initiatives are designed to reach out to Demat Account holders and potential investors, providing them with valuable information about Depository services, updates, precautions, best practices, grievance redressal systems, and other essential investor safeguards. The programmes are conducted in various languages, including English, Hindi, Marathi, and other regional languages to ensure widespread awareness and accessibility. NSDL commemorated International Women's Day celebrations this year by organising an investor awareness programme at SNDT Women's University, Mumbai, Maharashtra, which was attended by more than 300 girl students.

Market Ka Eklavya (MKE): In May 2022, the Honourable Finance Minister Smt. Nirmala Sitharaman launched NSDL's flagship online programme 'Market Ka Eklavya,' which educates and sensitises students to the need for financial planning to manage their money for their future. MKE is designed to help young people become the Eklavyas of the securities market. It aims to promote financial literacy and empower young people with the knowledge and skills they need to succeed in the securities market. The programme is committed to helping young people make informed investment decisions and build a strong foundation for their financial future. The programme is delivered online in Hindi, English, and other regional languages.

In 2022-2023, NSDL conducted 264 '*Market Ka Eklavya Programmes*' in 9 languages, impacting close to 16,000+ students. Close to 50% of the above participants were women.

Publications from NSDL: NSDL has made use of newsletters, books, and e-guides to create awareness among different investors. It publishes two monthly newsletters – 'The Financial Kaleidoscope' for investors and 'NSDL Update' for DPs and other business partners. It has published a book titled *NSDL Primer on Personal Finance* that provides step-by-step guidance to accumulating wealth through savings and investment. NSDL has made available an e-Guide for Demat Account Holders that provides investors with a comprehensive view of the capital markets, including intermediaries involved, and various products and services that NSDL offers. In addition, it has an information brochure for investors, FAQs on Demat accounts, and a booklet on the securities market. Most of the material is available in multiple languages.

Use of Social Media for Spreading Awareness and Education: During the fiscal year 2023, NSDL began using the official 'Instagram' account to reach out to the investor community and keep them informed of the recent developments taking place in the Capital Markets. With this, NSDL is now available on five social media platforms, namely LinkedIn, Twitter, Facebook, Instagram, and YouTube. NSDL publishes various key messages on a variety of investor-related topics, including videos on guidelines to become a prudent investor, Mutual Funds, e-voting, precautions to be taken while using social media, etc. NSDL also organises various quiz competitions on its social media platforms to encourage user participation and awareness on various aspects impacting investors.

XI. Metropolitical Stock Exchange (MSE)

Metropolitan Stock Exchange of India Ltd (MSE) is recognized by the Securities and Exchange Board of India (SEBI) under Section 4 of the Securities Contracts (Regulation) Act, 1956. The Exchange was declared a "recognized stock exchange" through the Ministry of Corporate Affairs, Govt. of India, on December 21, 2012.

'Information, Innovation, Education and Research' are the four bases of the unique market expansion philosophy used by MSE and maintain its mission of Financial-literacy-for-Financial Inclusion, as is conceived by the Government of India. The Exchange has cooperated with academic institutions of repute, media, trade bodies, international standards, and business experts for planning knowledge and awareness drives.

MSE believes in connecting with the investor community at large and helping them to become a 'Prudent Investor' and spread financial literacy amongst investors through Investor Awareness Programmes. MSE conducts Investor Awareness Program (IAPs).

They also provide a range of "Securities Market Common Booklets" in multiple Indian languages, making financial literacy accessible to a wider audience. These booklets cover essential topics and are designed to help investors from diverse linguistic backgrounds understand the basics of the market, empowering them with the knowledge required to navigate the complexities of investing.

MSE has participated in World Investor Week and has undertaken the following initiatives:

1. Do's and Don'ts in the Securities Market
2. Investment Mantras from the likes of Radhkrishna and Ramesh Damani, Ramdeo Agarwal, and Vijay Kedia
3. Kaun Banega Investor? A crossword for investors
4. Jargon of the day
5. Investor Awareness Videos

"Knowledge is that possession that no misfortune can destroy, no authority can revoke, and no enemy can control. This makes knowledge the greatest of all freedoms."

- Bryant H. McGill

Chapter 7

"Legacy of the Ledger: The Imperative Need of Institutionalising Processes and Maintaining Records"

In the sixth pivotal episode of my life's narrative, I delved deep into the art and science of one of the most important aspects of achieving any objective in life, which will unfold in this chapter. I had the opportunity to work with the Hyderabad (Sind) National Collegiate Board (HSNC Board), which is the management of our college, i.e., H. R. College of Commerce & Economics, where I am currently working as the Vice-Principal and Director of Placements.

I was working with the office of the Secretary, H(S)NCB, Principal Dinesh Panjwani, who is a renowned academician and a veteran administrator with over 30 years of experience as the Principal in three colleges. Though I was designated as an Associate, International Initiatives, and was expected to work on the Internationalisation of Higher Education for 14 prestigious colleges established and managed by the H(S)NC Board, I did not spend too much time on the assignment for the following reasons:

The pandemic was announced in 2020, and very few personnel were available in-person in the office.

The H(S)NC Board was granted permission to establish the prestigious HSNC University, Mumbai, a State Cluster University, with three grant-in-aid colleges as constituent colleges, which had consistently scored excellent NAAC grades. So, the three colleges - H. R. College (as the lead college), K. C. College, and Bombay Teachers' Training College became constituents of the HSNC University, Mumbai, by a notification of the Government of Maharashtra, dated 30 October 2019.

This meant that there were fewer people available to work on this project, and it presented an excellent opportunity to meet our goals. Most of the time was devoted to assisting the Secretary of the H(S)NCB in preparing the Detailed Project Report (DPR), which was a requirement of the Rashtriya Uchhatra Siksha Abhiyaan (RUSA), along with the team of Principals, Vice-Principals, and senior teachers. Much time was devoted to managing piles of paperwork, attending meetings, recording the minutes, participating in Zoom calls, and the like! And I ended up being the subject of ridicule among my colleagues!

For example, one of the senior lady professors (whom I don't wish to name) had the audacity to call me a 'glorified clerk.' I was hurt, and I approached Principal Panjwani with the question, "Sir, why do we have to be so meticulous about paperwork, processes, procedures, and signature sheets?"

He said, "Navinji, we are creating something for posterity; this University will live on beyond decades and outlast any of our lifetimes; it is our moral obligation to maintain true and fair records and institutionalise processes."

One day, when I was accompanying Principal Panjwani to the RUSA office, we received a call from the Joint Director, RUSA, requesting numerous documents from the colleges, such as NAAC certificates, ASHE registrations, the number of students enrolled, the number of sanctioned posts, the number of posts filled, vacant posts… the list was endless. That's when I understood the wisdom of Prin. Panjwani's insistence on maintaining records meticulously. We could easily provide the required information for all three colleges in no time. He looked at me and said, "Kyoon Navinji, ab boliye, isn't the need to institutionalise processes the need of the hour! Radhe Radhe?" He smiled.

Later, Prin. Panjwani had the honour of serving as the First Vice-Chancellor of HSNC University, Mumbai, and during his tenure, I was part of various committees of the University. I learned a lot about academic administration during this period. Whenever I went to him with an idea, he would be very encouraging about it. However, he would ask me very pertinent questions like, "Under which section of the Maharashtra Public Universities Act do we have the power to undertake such an activity? Have we prepared the relevant statutes, ordinances, or regulations for it? Only then would such proposals be placed before the relevant authorities of the University, and only when they are approved would those projects be undertaken." He would emphasise, "Process is very important; most good things are possible. However, we live in a democratic environment, and in administration, if you wish to succeed, it is best to always work within the prescribed processes."

I couldn't agree with him more, and I learned one of the most valuable lessons in life from him: the art and science of being process-driven and the importance of institutionalised systems. All this I could learn only from an administrator who, like Principal Panjwani, had the experience of working with government agencies and the expertise in generating systems and procedures so that they are no longer person-driven but system-driven once they are institutionalised. Another thing I learned was that all that you do in your lifetime is not just for your personal benefit; it constitutes a legacy for the future.

Thus, I learned to ignore the taunts and the gossip - and continued on my journey of learning the process of institutionalisation of processes and creating templates that would collate relevant data sets. On the face of it, it appears to be child's play, but, trust me, it requires a futuristic mode of thinking, which serves to broaden your vision.

During my tenure with the H(S)NC Board, I was consistently exposed to the intricate frameworks of educational administration, encompassing strategic planning, systematic record-keeping, and detailed documentation, and most importantly, the institutionalising processes. This experience provided me with an amazing insight: that the methodologies applied in the realm of education could be seamlessly applied to personal finance management as well. It was this realisation that inspired the conceptualisation of the Wealth Diary. Just as educational institutions meticulously maintain student records, track academic progress, and monitor financial health, individuals can also benefit from a structured approach to documenting their financial journey. The Wealth Diary is my endeavour to transpose the precision and foresight from the education sector into the world of personal finance, ensuring that individuals have a consolidated, comprehensive, and clear record of their financial assets, liabilities, goals, and progress.

Diya and I have always asked ourselves an important question: what is the ultimate use of all the money we earn, or the wealth that one possesses? Once you have your basic necessities fulfilled and have ensured a comfortable lifestyle for the family, what can the surplus money be used for? After long deliberation, we both agreed that the ultimate use of the wealth of any individual should be for charity and succession.

Charity allows you to contribute to society at large and to extend your influence beyond your immediate sphere, thus, creating a lasting impact. The joy of giving, of knowing that your hard-earned money is being used to make the world a better place, to provide opportunities for those less fortunate, is a reward in itself. However, it requires planning and financial management to ensure that your philanthropic goals are aligned with your financial capability.

On the other hand, wealth succession ensures that your hard-earned assets will be distributed according to your wishes and that your loved ones will be financially secure after you. Proper planning of estate and succession can prevent familial disputes and unnecessary legal hassles; and even reduce inheritance taxes. Again, careful financial record-keeping is crucial to ensure such a smooth succession.

Therefore, applying meticulous data standardisation in personal finance can enable you to plan for these outcomes effectively. You can track income, expenditures, investments, and savings, and plan for both short-term and long-term goals. By having a clear picture of your financial health, you can decide how much you can comfortably allocate towards charitable causes and what assets you would want to pass on to the next generation.

The concept of succession is customary. However, two essential elements should be in place for smooth succession: a proper record of assets and liabilities, and the testamentary intentions of the family member wishing to pass on the assets and/or liabilities. Hence, I suggest maintaining a "Wealth Diary," or as I like to call it, the "Blue Book." As per your preference, you may decide to call it the Red, Orange, Green, Black, White, Grey Book. This book of yours is a very personal document, and its colour code could resonate with all those who are 'insiders' and who are part of the inner circle of the family.

Managing your finances can be overwhelming, but keeping accurate and up-to-date records is essential to ensuring that your financial and legal obligations are met. By maintaining a single, organised record of all your financial and legal information, you can stay on top of your obligations, make informed decisions, and avoid costly mistakes.

This book is designed to provide safe storage of financial information that may be accessed by the family/spouse of the owner whenever needed. It ensures that the beneficiaries have access to all necessary information and details regarding the monetary and legal obligations, responsibilities, and avenues that may have been created or invested in. The information in this book is sensitive and confidential and also contains information about the various persons associated with various investments.

It is crucial that you keep this book confidential and safe, as it contains sensitive and personal information that should not be shared with anyone who does not have a legitimate reason to access it. Your personal financial and legal record book should be kept in a secure location that is accessible only to you or a trusted individual, such as a spouse or family member.

By investing the time and effort into maintaining the Blue Book, a personal financial and legal record, you can gain peace of mind and confidence in the fact that all pertinent legal and financial information is accessible to your loved ones at any time. This book is an invaluable resource for anyone who wants to take control of their financial and legal future and safely store precious personal information.

The Blue Book, a personal Diary of wealth, is a confidential document that records an individual's or family's financial information in a highly detailed and organised manner. It encapsulates sensitive information such as investment data, insurance details, real estate holdings, business interests, liabilities, and much more. Therefore, it needs to be handled with utmost care and confidentiality.

The contents of the Blue Book are personal in nature, often reflecting financial goals, strategies, successes and failures, and plans for the future.

Its disclosure could lead to unintended consequences, such as invasion of privacy, potential misuse of information, and even financial fraud in worst-case scenarios. Hence, the Blue Book should always be kept confidential, accessible only to the individual it pertains to, and any trusted advisers or family members who have been explicitly given access. The confidentiality of the Blue Book safeguards one's financial security and preserves the integrity of personal financial planning.

This book is like a key to your life, and if kept in the open, it can result in serious damage to you and your property. We strongly recommend that you keep this book in a secure place under lock and key with the utmost protection.

Chapter 8

The Blue Book - Physical or Digital

In the era of rapid digitalisation, where convenience meets efficiency, the decision to maintain one's Wealth Diary – my treasured 'Blue Book' – beckons a crucial choice: Do we embrace the tangible touch of paper or the seamless swipe of screens? Or perhaps, do we find a blend of both? This chapter delves into the merits and drawbacks of each mode, guiding you on a journey to find the most fitting medium for your financial records.

The "Blue Book" can be either physical or digital, depending on your preference, ease of use, and concerns about security.

A physical Blue Book is the traditional choice, and it can be appealing because it allows you to have a tangible record of your financial and legal information. This method can be more secure in some ways, as it does not rely on digital systems that could be vulnerable to cyber-attacks or technical failures. However, a physical book is susceptible to physical damage, such as fire or water damage, and it can also be lost or stolen.

A digital Blue Book, on the other hand, offers convenience and flexibility. You can easily update, create a backup, and access your information from anywhere. It is also easier to use search functions to find specific entries quickly. Additionally, digital records can be securely encrypted and protected by passwords, making them a secure choice if proper precautions are taken. However, the risk of cyber threats should be taken into account; so it is important to secure your digital Blue Book with strong passwords and perhaps two-factor authentication.

Hybrid solutions are also possible. You can maintain a physical Blue Book for the most crucial records and a digital version for easier access and updates. It is essential to ensure that both versions are securely stored and regularly updated.

Regardless of whether you choose a physical or digital format, the most critical factor is to ensure that the Blue Book is kept safe, secure, and up-to-date. It should also be easily accessible to trusted individuals who would need this information in case of an emergency.

A video message can be created and made a part of the Blue Book. I strongly believe in leveraging existing technology to achieve the objective, which in this case is to properly and accurately document personal financial matters.

Leaving a video message for your loved ones can be a deeply personal and meaningful gesture. It allows you to express your feelings, wishes and hopes for your family in a way that written words might not fully capture. A video message can provide comfort, guidance, and reassurance to your loved ones in difficult times and serve as a lasting memory of your love and presence in their lives.

Here are some considerations and steps for creating a meaningful video message:

1. **Choose a Quiet and Comfortable Setting:** Select a place where you feel comfortable and relaxed. The setting should be quiet and free from distractions.
2. **Plan Your Message:** Before you start recording, plan what you want to say. This doesn't mean you need a full script; you may just jot down the key points you want to convey.
3. **Speak from the Heart:** It is essential to be sincere in your video message. Speak from the heart and share your feelings, hopes, and wishes for your loved ones.
4. **Provide Guidance:** If you are leaving a video message as part of your legacy, you might consider sharing life lessons, words of wisdom, or guidance for future challenges.
5. **Consider including Practical Information:** If you're comfortable doing so, you could use part of your video message to discuss your

financial or legal affairs, particularly if this information is crucial for your loved ones.

6. **Keep it Positive:** While the context might be sombre, try to keep the tone of your message positive. Talk about your love for them, the happiness they've brought you, and your wishes for their future happiness.
7. **Check the Video Quality:** Ensure that the video and audio quality are good. It is important that your loved ones can clearly see and hear you.
8. **Store the Video Securely:** Once you're satisfied with your message, make sure it is stored securely and in a location where your loved ones can access it when necessary.
9. **Update as Needed:** Life changes, and your feelings, thoughts, and circumstances can evolve. Consider updating your video message as major life events occur or as your feelings shift.

Remember, the goal of your video message isn't to cause sadness or distress but to leave a lasting legacy of your love, advice, and wishes for your loved ones. It is a special gift that they can treasure for years to come.

You may consider creating multiple video messages for different occasions. This is a thoughtful way of communicating with your loved ones during significant life events or emergencies. Such messages can provide comfort, guidance, and important information. Video messages can be created for the following occasions:

1. **In Case of Death:** This video message could encompass your final goodbyes, your reflections on life, and your hopes and dreams for your loved ones' futures. You might also choose to share details about your will and other arrangements you've made.
2. **In Case of Emergency:** This could be a more practical video in which you outline crucial information, like your medical history, your doctor's contact information, where important documents like health insurance cards are kept, etc. This could be invaluable in a situation where you are unable to communicate this information yourself.
3. **Annual Message:** You might consider creating an annual video message reflecting on the past year, expressing your love and appreciation for

your family, and sharing your hopes for the coming year. This can serve as a beautiful keepsake and chronicle of your life.

4. **Special Occasions:** You could create video messages intended for specific moments in your loved ones' lives, such as graduations, marriages, anniversaries, birthdays, or the birth of a child. These messages can provide a way for you to be "present" during these important milestones, even when you're no longer around.

In creating these messages, it is crucial to store them securely and in a place where your loved ones will be able to access them at the appropriate time. It is also important to regularly update these messages as your circumstances, feelings, and thoughts evolve.

Remember, these video messages serve multiple purposes: they're not just a way to relay practical information but also to express your love, share your wisdom, and leave a lasting legacy for your loved ones to treasure.

Indeed, while the Blue Book serves as an organised and comprehensive record of your personal financial and legal information, video messages offer an additional layer of depth, context, and emotion that can prove to be invaluable.

1. **Emotions:** Video messages can capture the nuances of your personality and emotions in a way that written words may not. Your tone of voice, expressions, and body language add layers of meaning to your message. Leaving a video message for your loved ones allows you to express your love, care, and concern in a personal, direct way. It provides comfort and a sense of closeness and can be a source of strength to them in challenging times.

2. **Knowledge and Skills Transfer:** A video message is a powerful tool for imparting knowledge and skills, especially when it comes to managing wealth. You could use video messages to explain complex concepts, talk about your experiences, provide tips and insights, and share your philosophy on wealth management. This could be particularly useful if the person who will be handling the wealth in an emergency is not familiar with your financial landscape or lacks experience in managing wealth.

3. **Contextual Information:** The Blue Book provides the 'what' and 'where' of your financial assets and legal information. A video message can supplement this by providing the 'why' and 'how'. You can explain the reasoning behind certain financial decisions, your future plans for certain assets, or how you envision the wealth being used or distributed.
4. **Ease of Understanding:** For some people, especially those who are visual or auditory learners, a video message can be easier to understand than written information.
5. **Ensuring Continuity:** By sharing your insights, you'll help ensure that your wealth is managed in a way that aligns with your values and intentions, providing a sense of continuity.

Actually, while the Blue Book and video messages serve different purposes, together they offer a more comprehensive and powerful legacy: one that combines practical knowledge with emotional wisdom and personal insights.

In the subsequent pages, we've provided space for you to create a QR code link to a video. This video is intended for a specific family member or loved one to view in case of an exigency. However, the content of this video is crucial!

Creating such a video for your loved ones can be an intensely personal and emotional task. You'll need to consider carefully the messages you wish to impart. Here are some elements you might want to include as you plan and create this video:

The content of such a video will depend on its intended purpose. Assuming this video is to be viewed in a situation where you cannot communicate directly due to an accident, serious illness, or passing, you might consider including the following elements:

1. **Affectionate Greetings and Emotional Support:** Start the video with a loving greeting and reassure the viewer that although you're not physically present, your thoughts and love remain with them. You might want to express your trust in them and their ability to handle the situation.

2. **Overview and Purpose:** Explain briefly why you have created the video. This might involve explaining the situation you envisioned when you made the video.
3. **Practical Advice and Instructions:** This could be the bulk of the content. Provide any information, advice, or instructions that the viewer might need. This might involve details about finances, contacts, legal documents, your wishes regarding medical treatment, or other important information.
4. **Personal Messages:** Share personal messages for your loved ones. This could involve expressing your feelings for them, sharing hopes for their futures, offering words of advice, or simply reminiscing about happy memories.
5. **Closure:** Conclude the video on a positive note. You might want to express your love again, share some words of comfort, or give a final piece of advice. You might also reassure them that they have the strength and resources to deal with the situation.

Remember to keep your tone calm and comforting in the videos. Despite the serious nature of the content, the video should ideally provide solace and not cause additional stress. It is not easy to strike this balance, so consider drafting a script or key points beforehand to ensure that you cover everything you want to convey.

Remember, this video is essentially a part of your legacy, and it could be one of the last personal interactions your loved ones have with you. Make sure it represents you accurately and affectionately.

Now that you have decided what you want to convey to your loved ones in the video, some of you may want to learn how to create a QR code for the video that you have recorded for your loved ones.

Creating a QR code for a video involves a few steps. Here are the general guidelines:

1. **Upload the Video to a Platform**: If your video isn't already online, you will need to upload it to a platform that hosts video content. This could be a social media site like YouTube, Vimeo, or Google Drive (Please remember to keep the setting as 'ANYONE WITH THE

LINK CAN VIEW'), or Dropbox. Once the video is uploaded, make sure it is set to be viewable by anyone with the link.

2. **Copy the Video Link:** Once your video is uploaded and its privacy settings are adjusted, you can copy its URL.
3. **Use a QR Code Generator:** There are many free QR code generators available online such as QR Code Monkey, QR Code Generator, or QR Stuff. Go to one of these sites, and select the option to create a QR code for a URL.
4. **Paste the Video Link:** In the field provided by the QR Code Generator, paste the URL of your video. The generator will then create a QR code that, when scanned, will take the user directly to your video.
5. **Download and Print the QR Code:** Most QR Code Generators will allow you to download the generated QR code as an image file. Once downloaded, you can print this image and include it in your book or any other physical media.

Please remember to test the QR code by scanning it with a smartphone to ensure that it redirects to your video properly. It is a good idea to have someone else test it as well, just to be sure it works for different devices.

Also, bear in mind that not all online platforms are considered permanent repositories, so it is important to choose a platform that you expect to remain available for the long-term. If the online video is removed or the platform is shut down, the QR code will no longer link to the video.

Now that you have created a QR code, take a printout of the QR code and stick it on the page provided for it. Once again, scan the QR code and test it before you paste it in your Blue Book.

A letter for the person/s authorised to access your Video:

To, _____________,

If you are reading this page of my book, it signifies that I, ________________________, hold immense trust in you and seek to provide guidance during challenging times. If this message has come into your hands, it means I am currently unable to communicate due to an accident, death, or other exigency that has left me incommunicado. Therefore, it is of utmost importance that you carefully watch the video accessed via the QR code below and proceed as directed.

To access the video, open the camera application on your phone and scan the QR Code. If you are unfamiliar with scanning a QR code, open Google Lens, scan the QR code, and a link will appear. Simply click on the link to view the video.

Space to Paste a QR Code

I love you, and even though I might not be physically there with you, this digital video will provide the necessary guidance to help you navigate this difficult time more easily.

While I cannot predict when or if I'll be back soon, I take solace in knowing that you have been taken care of in my absence.

Yours lovingly, ____ (Signature)

____ [Your Name]

Chapter 09

The Importance of Saving Essential Documents on the Cloud

As we navigate a progressively digital age, the imperative of safeguarding our essential documents takes precedence. Storing them on the cloud isn't merely a tech-savvy choice; it's a proactive measure ensuring accessibility, security, and peace of mind. In this chapter, we illuminate the manifold advantages and challenges of cloud storage and emphasise its importance in preserving our invaluable records.

In today's digital age, it is crucial to keep all your important documents organised and accessible. Documents like your PAN Card, Driving Licence, Aadhar Card, and passport are essential for various purposes, from opening a bank account to travelling internationally. Losing these documents can cause significant stress and inconvenience, and getting replacements can be a time-consuming and cumbersome process. Hence, it is imperative to keep them safe and also easily accessible.

Options for Storing Digital Documents

1. **Cloud Storage:** Cloud storage services like Google Drive or OneDrive allow you to store your documents on the Internet, making them accessible from any device with an Internet connection.
2. **E-mail:** Another option is to send the scanned documents to yourself or a trusted family member via email. This way, the documents are

stored in the email account and can be accessed from any device that can log into the email account. However, these days email accounts require two-factor authentication, i.e., a password and a confirmation from your phone that you are attempting to access the email or a code, or it will prompt you to click on a number on your phone. This added layer of security ensures that only authorised individuals can access the email account, but it can also make it more challenging to access the documents quickly in an emergency.

Why Save Important Documents on the Cloud?

1. **Ease of Access:** Once your documents are stored on the Cloud, you can access them anytime, anywhere, as long as you have an internet connection. This is particularly useful for frequent travellers or those living abroad.
2. **Safety and Security:** Physical documents can get lost, damaged, or stolen. On the other hand, documents stored on the Cloud are safe from natural disasters, theft, or accidental loss.
3. **Sharing with Family Members:** Storing your essential documents on the Cloud makes it easier to share them with family members when necessary. For instance, if a family member needs to access your documents in an emergency, they can do so with your permission, without having to search through your belongings.
4. **Reduction of Clutter:** Storing documents on the Cloud helps reduce physical clutter. You don't need to maintain a bulky file of important papers.
5. **Ease of Updating:** It is easier to update digital copies of documents. For example, if you change your address and update your Aadhar Card, you can quickly replace the old document with the new one on the Cloud.

How to Save Important Documents on the Cloud?

1. **Scanning:** The first step is to create digital copies of all your important documents. Use a scanner or a scanning app on your smartphone to create high-quality digital copies.

2. **Organising:** Create folders for different categories of documents. For example, you can have one folder for government-issued IDs, another for financial documents, and so on.
3. **Storing:** Upload the scanned documents to a Cloud storage service like Google Drive or OneDrive. Make sure to organise the documents in the folders you created.
4. **Sharing:** Share the folders or specific documents with family members or others who may need access. Most Cloud storage services allow you to share documents or folders with specific email addresses and set permissions for viewing or editing.
5. **Updating:** Regularly update the documents stored on the Cloud. If there are any changes to your personal information or if you acquire new important documents, make sure to upload them to the Cloud.

Conclusion

In today's digital age, storing important documents on the Cloud is a smart and practical way to keep them safe, organised, and easily accessible. It also makes it easier to share them with family members when necessary. So, take the time to digitise, organise, and store all your essential documents on the cloud. It will give you peace of mind and make your life easier and better organised.

Section II
THE WEALTH DIARY

This section, presenting the Wealth Diary, is yours and yours alone. It is a very personal and extremely important document. While we have titled it "The Wealth Diary," or as I like to call it, my Blue Book, you are free to call it whatever feels most comfortable for you. Regardless of the title, this section will serve as a comprehensive repository of all your personal, financial, and legal information.

How to Use This Section

1. **Be Thorough:** Take your time to fill out each section carefully. Don't rush through it. Make sure to include all relevant information.
2. **Be Clear:** Don't assume that your spouse or authorised personnel will understand everything you wish to say. If there is any chance of confusion, provide necessary clarifications.
3. **Use Notes:** Whenever in doubt, mark an item or question with an asterisk (*) or a hashtag (#) mark and elaborate upon it in the notes pages at the end of the section.

Confidentiality

I know I have repeated it several times, but remember that the information you record here is extremely sensitive. Ensure your own and your family's security by storing the Diary in a protected location, in a safe, a locked filing cabinet, or a secure digital location that only you and your designated trusted individuals can access.

Final Note

Completing this section may feel like an overwhelming task due to the sheer volume and nature of the information. However, doing it thoroughly will provide you and your loved ones with peace of mind since you will be sure that everything is organised and accessible when needed.

Now, let's begin. Remember, take your time, and be thorough and clear.

Declaration

I, ________________________(Full Name) , hereby acknowledge and understand that "The Wealth Diary" ________________ [Colour] Book (hereafter referred to as "The Book") is a tool for recording my personal financial information. I recognise the sensitive nature of the data contained within the Book and the risks associated with documenting such information in a consolidated manner.

I am using The Book willingly and at my own risk. I fully understand and accept that the safekeeping, storage, and protection of The Book falls solely under my responsibility. I am aware of the potential consequences resulting from misuse, loss, or mishandling of the information, and I commit to taking all necessary measures to prevent such occurrences.

I hereby authorise the following individuals (Authorised Persons) as follows:

- Name: ______________________________ Mobile No: ______________
- Name: ______________________________ Mobile No: ______________
- Name: ______________________________ Mobile No: ______________
- Name: ______________________________ Mobile No: ______________

to access the contents of The Book. I understand that any unauthorised access to The Book is a breach of my personal privacy and may result in legal action.

I acknowledge that Dr. Navin M. Punjabi, the author of The Book, or any associated entity involved in the creation, production, or distribution of The Book, shall not be held liable or responsible for any misuse, theft, loss, or mishandling of the information contained within it or of The Book itself. I recognise that it is my duty and responsibility to ensure the safety, confidentiality, and appropriate use of this Book and the information therein.

Signed:

[Your Name] _______________

Date:

[Date]_______________

Components of The Book

Essential Details: The page containing personal information of yourself and your family, your service along with your business details, as details of technical devices/logins, is of utmost sensitivity. Safeguarding this information is essential to protect yourself and the persons who can access it against unauthorised access and potential risks.

Investment Records: The Book maintains a detailed account of all investments, including stocks, bonds, mutual funds, real estate properties, and any other financial instruments. It records crucial information such as costs, dividends, interest rates, and relevant documentation.

Budgeting and Expenses Tracking: The Book aids in budgeting and tracking expenses by documenting regular expenditures, such as utility bills, mortgage payments, insurance premiums, and discretionary spending. It helps individuals and families evaluate their spending habits, identify areas for improvement, and make informed decisions about the allocation of resources.

Estate Planning: The Book plays a vital role in estate planning by recording important details related to wills, trusts, and inheritance. It helps ensure that the family's assets are properly distributed according to the individual's or family's wishes after their demise.

Financial Goals and Strategies: The Book serves as a platform for setting financial goals and documenting strategies to achieve them. It may include long-term objectives like retirement planning, education funding, debt reduction plans, and investment strategies tailored to individual risk tolerance and financial aspirations.

Names and Mobile Numbers of Trusted Professionals and Friends: The Book is more than just a repository for financial details; it is a nexus of invaluable contacts that have, over time, become akin to family. It holds the names and mobile numbers of key associates, each specialising in their respective fields – be it a Chartered Accountant (CA) for financial intricacies, a Company Secretary (CS) for corporate guidance, a lawyer for legal counsel, or a doctor for health advisories. These individuals aren't just professionals; they are confidantes, each one of them having built a rapport that exceeds mere transactional interactions. Their inclusion in The Book signifies their importance in the fabric of one's life, ensuring that at times of need, whether it is a financial query or a health concern, trusted advice is just a call away. In the ever-evolving journey of life, The Book serves as a beacon, lighting the way with familiar faces and trusted voices.

Digital Assets: The Book is an embodiment of the modern age, blending traditional wealth management with the digital sphere. It not only captures vital contacts who have grown close to the family but also securely preserves digital assets, including passwords for social media platforms like Instagram, LinkedIn, and Facebook, and essential email accounts. In today's interconnected world, your network truly mirrors your net worth. These platforms represent more than just digital footprints; they encompass memories, professional accomplishments, relationships, and invaluable contacts. The connections we make and the lives we touch, often without our knowing it, can have far-reaching impact. You never truly know the extent of the positive influence you've had on someone until a day comes when they step forward in your hour of need. The Book is not just a guardian of wealth but a curator of connections, ensuring that, even in unforeseen circumstances, one's legacy and network remain accessible and intact.

Frequently Asked Questions about The Book

1. **What is the motive of The Book?**

   The primary motive of The Book is to serve as a comprehensive guide, consolidating all essential financial details that a family might need. In the face of unforeseen circumstances, it is imperative that family members can seamlessly access, comprehend, and, if necessary, amend pertinent financial information. This book acts as a one-stop repository, ensuring that financial transitions and decisions can be made smoothly without the added stress of locating and deciphering scattered or ambiguous details. Whether it is for routine financial management or in times of urgency, The Book aims to empower families with the knowledge and organisation needed to handle financial matters with confidence and ease.

2. **How does The Book act as a guide for your dependents and loved ones?**

   The Book contains all the information required to understand one's personal belongings, professional contacts, and financials, and it is available collated in a single document.

3. **Is this book for an individual or a family?**

   The Book has been composed keeping in mind a family of two adults with three children, and their parents living with them. The author recognises that most couples today have one or, at most, two children. Therefore, the space designated for the third child can alternatively be used as a 'Remarks' column to record additional details. Similarly, if your parents aren't living with you, their designated space can be employed for documenting other essential information. For those who find The Book's assets documentation space limited, congratulations on achieving High Net Worth Individual (HNI) status! You can most likely afford a Wealth Manager, at this stage. Take the provided template, and with your Wealth Manager's assistance, customise it to accommodate both your domestic and international assets. The book aims to cater to the average Indian citizen, ensuring that their wealth is well-managed and recorded.

4. **How is The Book to be used?**

   One must identify the concerned/relevant chapters first, start filling out them, make all the entries, write the extra information in the notes, create a digital copy of the information that their family needs to know, and share a QR code of that information in the book.

5. **Why are so many questions repeated in different sections?**

   This book has been made keeping in mind differing financial literacy levels. First of all, it is tailored for your personal comprehension and reference. We understand that finances and related details can be complex, and revisiting certain points ensures clarity and reinforces memory. Secondly, the book has been structured keeping in mind its potential use by family members in times of exigency. It is paramount that in such critical moments, anyone accessing the information can understand it easily and navigate it. Given that not everyone authorised to access this book might possess the same level of financial acumen or familiarity with your personal arrangements, repetition acts as a safeguard, ensuring that crucial details aren't overlooked, and the intended message is conveyed with clarity each time.

6. **Why is it important to maintain a personal financial and legal record?**

   It is important for effective financial management, informed decision-making, meeting legal obligations, and providing a secure and accessible repository of information for you and your loved ones.

7. **Who should know about the existence of The Book?**

   Only trusted individuals must know about the existence of The Book—those who will require this information in order to access the financials of the creator. One must let their trusted people know about the existence of The Book and its location.

8. **Who should have access to my Book?**

   Only one or two trusted individuals should have access to The Book; they must be of sound mind and capable of making decisions on your behalf.

9. **Where should The Book be placed to keep it secure?**

   The physical copy of The Book must be kept safely in a locker or at a trusted source that is not easily accessible to anyone. One must have multiple levels of security to gain access to this document. As The Book requires periodic updates, you may want to store it at your residence or workplace under lock and key or in a secured cupboard.

10. **How regularly must The Book be updated?**

    The Book must be updated at least every quarter of the year or based on your needs. It is your book, and it may be updated as frequently as you deem necessary.

11. **How can the QR Code mentioned be attached in The Book?**

    On a private network, add the documents or any information you wish to pass on and which can be contained in that network. Create a QR Code of the address of the network and paste it into the book.

12. **What should the Notes Section include?**

    It may include any additional information or working notes to the final copy provided in The Book. It is your book, and you can write any message or notes on how to use this book or any other important details as per your need.

13. **What kind of property details one should write in the Property Section?**

    The Property Section must include the Date of Purchase/Rent/Lease, Amount of Purchase, Type of Property, Location of the Property, Previous/Actual Owner of the Property, and any disputable information that is important.

14. **In case of any emergency, whom should you contact?**

    Any individual mentioned in The Book under the emergency contacts is to be contacted in case of a medical emergency or any other emergency you can foresee.

15. **Can I store my "Blue Book" digitally, or is a physical copy necessary?**

    A physical copy must be kept in a secured digital environment. It must have multiple modes of security, such as biometric, retinal, alphanumeric passcodes, etc. Also, ensure that it requires a physical key plugged in to access the document.

16. **What should I do if I lose my "Blue Book" or it gets stolen?**

    Erase all the information, change your passwords, and contact your respective banks to hold on to all transactions. Also, report the theft to the nearest Police Station. However, it is strongly recommended that you take utmost care of The Book and not lose it under any circumstances.

17. **Can I use a password manager or digital storage for my "Blue Book"?**

    We highly advise you not to rely on a single mode of protection for securing your Blue Book.

18. **Should I keep copies of legal documents in The Book, such as Wills and Powers of Attorney?**

    Yes, an individual must attach copies of the relevant documents in The Book for reference. Also, the location of the original documents.

19. **What is to be done with the old records of "The Book"?**

    One can keep updating in a new book, overwrite the existing content, keep no traces of the past, or put an asterisk mark and update the new details in the notes section.

20. **Can I add additional Sections or customise The Book to suit my specific needs?**

    Yes, you can customise the digital copy of The Book as per your needs and requirements. In the future, new digital assets like UPI Lite may come up, and you may want to record its newer login credentials.

21. **Are there any legal considerations I should keep in mind when maintaining the "Blue Book"?**

    Yes, there are legal considerations to keep in mind when maintaining a personal financial and legal record like The Book. Here are a few important points:

- **Privacy and Confidentiality:** The information contained in the book is sensitive and confidential, including personal, financial, and legal details. It is crucial to keep the book secure and limit access to trusted individuals alone to protect your privacy.
- **Compliance with Data Protection Laws:** Depending on your jurisdiction, there may be data protection laws and regulations in place that govern the collection, storage, and sharing of personal information. Ensure that you comply with applicable laws and take necessary measures to protect personal data.
- **Estate Planning and Wills:** The Book can be an essential resource for estate planning and drafting a Will. It can help your loved ones understand your financial affairs and locate important documents, ensuring your wishes are carried out effectively.
- **Legal Documentation:** Your "Blue Book" may contain copies of legal documents such as contracts, deeds, wills, powers of attorney, or insurance policies. It is important to ensure these documents are valid, up-to-date, and compliant with legal requirements.
- **Digital Assets and Online Accounts:** With the increasing prevalence of digital assets and online accounts, it is important to consider the legal aspects of managing and accessing these accounts. Include instructions and necessary information in The Book to facilitate their management and transfer in accordance with applicable laws and terms of service.

22. **Shall I give names of trusted people at the workplace?**

Yes. The workplace forms a significant part of one's life, and yet, families might not be aware of the key figures in that sphere. By listing trusted individuals, you are ensuring that your spouse or dependents have a direct line to people who understand the intricacies of your professional world. This becomes especially crucial in unexpected circumstances. Those listed can provide insights into HR policies, entitlements, benefits, and other specifics that your spouse might be unaware of. They can also assist in navigating any professional commitments or projects that are underway. Remember, the aim of The Book is to ease the process of managing affairs during challenging times, and this inclusion undoubtedly furthers that objective.

23. **Why are we recording details of House Help and Drivers?**

    It is very important to maintain a record of their identities and backgrounds for security purposes. By recording the details of house help and drivers, you are ensuring the safety and security of your household. In case of any unforeseen incident, having their details on hand can be vital for communication, verification, or even for legal procedures. Additionally, they often become integral parts of our daily lives, being privy to our routines, habits, and sometimes even our financial details. Having their information in The Book ensures that your family has an organised record of everyone closely associated with your domestic life, which can be invaluable in emergencies or any other circumstances where you need to contact or verify the identities of these individuals.

24. **What is a Master Word Document of Passwords?**

    It is a repository of all your passwords, be it social media accounts or any other online portal that requires a sign-in with a password. Storing passwords in a Master Word Document, while convenient, poses significant security risks. If accessed, this single document can offer intruders the keys to an individual's entire digital existence, right from banking to social media. Therefore, if one chooses to use such a method, it is imperative to secure the document with a robust password. However, for heightened security and efficiency, it is recommended that you utilise dedicated password managers like LastPass or 1Password, which not only store but also generate strong passwords, all while ensuring encrypted protection. Moreover, enabling two-factor authentication on accounts provides an additional layer of safety, making unauthorised access even more challenging. It is up to individuals to decide if they wish to record the password in the concerned section of the book, prepare a Master Word Document of all passwords, or use a service provider to help you store the same. The logic is that you yourself need to remember the accounts and also let your loved ones know about them so that they can access your accounts and documents when you are no longer around.

PART 1:

1. PERSONAL INFORMATION

PERSONAL INFORMATION	FULL NAME (First, Middle, Last Name)	DATE OF BIRTH	PLACE OF BIRTH
Self			
Spouse			
Child 1			
Child 2			
Child 3			
Father			
Mother			

IDENTITY	NATIONALITY	BLOOD GROUP	MARKS ON BODY, IF ANY	MEDICAL CONDITION
Self				
Spouse				
Child 1				
Child 2				
Child 3				
Father				
Mother				

VACCINATION DETAILS	NAME OF THE VACCINE	FIRST DOZE	SECOND DOZE	BOOSTER DOZE
Self				
Spouse				
Child 1				
Child 2				
Child 3				
Father				
Mother				

MOBILE DETAILS	MOBILE NO	HANDSET MAKE & IMEI NO	PIN/PATTERN
Self			
Spouse			
Child 1			
Child 2			
Child 3			
Father			
Mother			

If lost, you can get your handset blocked or unblocked https://www.ceir.gov.in/Home/index.jsp

LAPTOP	BRAND AND MAKE	SERIAL NO	PIN/PATTERN
Self			
Spouse			
Child 1			
Child 2			
Child 3			
Father			
Mother			

EMAIL DETAILS	EMAIL ADDRESS	PASSWORD	MOBILE LINKED
Self			
Spouse			
Child 1			
Child 2			
Child 3			
Father			
Mother			

ALTERNATE EMAIL	EMAIL ADDRESS	PASSWORD	MOBILE LINKED
Self			
Spouse			
Child 1			
Child 2			
Child 3			
Father			
Mother			

IDENTITY DOCUMENTS	PAN	AADHAR	VOTER ID
Self			
Spouse			
Child 1			
Child 2			
Child 3			
Father			
Mother			

IDENTITY DOCUMENTS	DRIVING LICENCE	ISSUE DATE	EXPIRY DATE
Self			
Spouse			
Child 1			
Child 2			
Child 3			
Father			
Mother			

IDENTITY	PASSPORT	ISSUE DATE	EXPIRY DATE
Self			
Spouse			
Child 1			
Child 2			
Child 3			
Father			
Mother			

LEGAL MATTER	ACTIVE CASES PLAINTIFF	ACTIVE CASES DEFENDANT	POWER OF ATTORNEY
Self			
Spouse			
Child 1			
Child 2			
Child 3			
Father			
Mother			

2. Important Personnel

TRUSTED INDIVIDUALS AT WORKPLACE	
Name	
Primary Mobile No	
Primary email Address	
Address	
Name	
Primary Mobile No	

TRUSTED INDIVIDUALS AT WORKPLACE	
Primary email Address	
Address	
CHARTERED ACCOUNTANT (CA)	
Name	
Primary Mobile Number	
Primary email Address	
Address	
LAWYER	
Name	
Primary Mobile Number	
Primary email Address	
Address	
INSURANCE CONSULTANT	
Name	
Primary Mobile Number	
Primary email Address	
Company Name & Address	

TRUSTED INDIVIDUALS AT WORKPLACE	
FAMILY DOCTOR	
Name	
Primary Mobile Number	
Primary email Address	
Address of the Hospital/Clinic	
COMPANY SECRETARY	
Name	
Primary Mobile Number	
Primary email Address	
Address	
OTHER PROFESSIONAL	
Name	
Primary Mobile Number	
Primary email Address	
Address	

3. HOUSE UTILITY ESSENTIALS

	ELECTRICITY	GAS	WIFI/TV
Identification Number			
Provider			
Mode of Payment			
Mobile Number for OTP			
Security Code/ Key/Question			

4. HOUSEHELP & ASSOCIATES DETAILS

	HOUSE HELP 1	HOUSE HELP 2
Name		
Contact Number		
Aadhar No.		
Part-time/Full-time		
Service Provided		
Reference		

5. SOCIAL MEDIA

SOCIAL MEDIA SELF- DETAILS	FACEBOOK	INSTAGRAM	TWITTER (X)	LINKEDIN
Username				
Password				
E-mail address for OTP				
Mobile Number for OTP				
Security Code/ Key/Question				

SOCIAL MEDIA SPOUSE - DETAILS	FACEBOOK	INSTAGRAM	TWITTER (X)	LINKEDIN
Username				
Password				
E-mail address for OTP				
Mobile Number for OTP				
Security Code/ Key/Question				

SOCIAL MEDIA CHILD 1 - DETAILS	FACEBOOK	INSTAGRAM	TWITTER (X)	LINKEDIN
Username				
Password				
E-mail address for OTP				
Mobile Number for OTP				
Security Code/ Key/Question				

SOCIAL MEDIA CHILD 2 - DETAILS	FACEBOOK	INSTAGRAM	TWITTER (X)	LINKEDIN
Username				
Password				
E-mail address for OTP				
Mobile Number for OTP				
Security Code/ Key/Question				

SOCIAL MEDIA CHILD 3 - DETAILS	FACEBOOK	INSTAGRAM	TWITTER (X)	LINKEDIN
Username				
Password				
E-mail address for OTP				
Mobile Number for OTP				
Security Code/ Key/Question				

SOCIAL MEDIA FATHER - DETAILS	FACEBOOK	INSTAGRAM	TWITTER (X)	LINKEDIN
Username				
Password				
E-mail address for OTP				
Mobile Number for OTP				
Security Code/ Key/Question				

SOCIAL MEDIA MOTHER-DETAILS	FACEBOOK	INSTAGRAM	TWITTER (X)	LINKEDIN
Username				
Password				
E-mail address for OTP				
Mobile Number for OTP				
Security Code/ Key/Question				

6. WARDS' SCHOOL/COLLEGE DETAILS

	CHILD 1	CHILD 2	CHILD 3
Name of the Institution			
Contact Number			
E-mail Address			
Emergency Contact - Name			
Emergency Contact - Contact Number			

	CHILD 1	CHILD 2	CHILD 3
Emergency Contact - Designation			
Address of the Institution			
Portal Username			
Portal Password			
Portal OTP email address			
Portal OTP Mobile Number			
Portal OTP Security Question			

7. MOTOR VEHICLE DETAILS

	VEHICLE 1	VEHICLE 2
Brand		
Model		
Year of Purchase		
Vehicle No.		
Registration Certificate (RC)		
Engine No.		
Chassis No.		
Pollution Under Control Paper, Location and Date		
Vehicle loan if any		
Name of the Bank		
Loan A/C No		

	VEHICLE 1	VEHICLE 2
Relationship Manager Name		
Mobile No		
Username/ID		
Password		
Insurance Company		
Policy No		
Start Date		
End Date		
Agent Name		
Agent Contact Details		
Roadside Breakdown Assistance Contact		

8. AUTOPAY - FASTAG

Vehicle make and No		
Operator/ Bank		
Username		
Password		
Security Question		
E-mail address for OTP		
Mobile Number for OTP		
Bank		
Account No.		
Debit/Credit Card No.		

9. BUSINESS / COMPANY DETAILS

	SELF	SPOUSE
Name of the Company		
Address		
E-mail address for OTP		
Mobile Number for OTP		
Official e-mail address		
Official Mobile Number		
GST Number		
MCA Login Number		
TAN Number		
DIN Number		
CIN Number		
TIN Number		
HR DETAILS		
Details	**SELF**	**SPOUSE**
Name		
Primary Mobile Number		
Primary e-mail address		
Other Details		

1. EMPLOYMENT DETAILS

Name of the Company		
Designation		
Year of Joining		
Type of Employment		
Annual Salary		
Name of the Reporting Manager		
Contact Number of the Reporting Manager		
E-mail Address of the Reporting Manager		
Income Tax Identification Number (ITIN)		
Registered OTP Mobile Number		
Registered OTP e-mail address		

Name of the Company		
Tax Identification Number (TIN)		
Registered OTP Mobile Number		
Registered OTP e-mail address		
Professional Tax Number		
Registered OTP Mobile Number		
Registered OTP e-mail address		
Any Other Employment Benefits		
Name of the HR		
Mobile Number of the HR		
E-mail Address of the HR		

Name of the Company		
If Group Life Insurance Yes, then refer to Insurance Section		
If Group Health Insurance Yes, refer to Health Insurance Section		
If EPF yes, refer to EPF Section		
If Pension Provided refer to Notes Section which type of pension, whether commuted or not.		
If NPS is transferred to Government is Yes, then refer to NPS Section.		

2. IMPORTANT PORTALS DETAILS:

INCOME TAX PORTAL SELF	
Username/ID	
Password	
Remarks	
INCOME TAX PORTAL SPOUSE	
Username/ID	
Password	
Remarks	
INCOME TAX PORTAL FATHER	
Username/ID	
Password	
Remarks	
INCOME TAX PORTAL MOTHER	
Username/ID	
Password	
Remarks	
GST PORTAL	
Username/ID	
Password	
Remarks	

INCOME TAX PORTAL SELF	
TDS PORTAL	
Username/ID	
Password	
Remarks	
PROFESIONAL TAX PORTAL	
Username/ID	
Password	
Remarks	
INDEPENDENT DIRECTOR PORTAL	
Username/ID	
Password	
Remarks	
MCA PORTAL	
Username/ID	
Password	
Remarks	
ANY OTHER PORTAL	
Username/ID	
Password	
Remarks	

3. ENTERTAINMENT SUBSCRIPTIONS/MEMBERSHIPS

Operator		
Username		
Password		
Security Question		
E-mail address for OTP		
Mobile Number for OTP		
Bank		
Account No.		
Debit/Credit Card No.		
AutoPay (Yes/No)		

4. CLUB MEMBERSHIPS

CLUB NAME	MEMBERSHIP NO	VALIDITY	REMARK E.G. NAME OF THE P. MEMBER / AFFILIATIONS

5. MEMBERSHIP PROFESSIONAL BODIES

NAME	MEMBERSHIP NO	VALIDITY	USERNAME/ ID	PASSWORD

PART 2: FINANCIAL INFORMATION

1. MOBILE WALLETS/UPI

UPI	SELF	SPOUSE
Service Provider 1 Name: e.g Gapy, Phone Pe, Amazon Pay, Mobikwick		
UPI ID / Virtual Payment Address (VPA)		
Username		
Password		
Security Question		
OTP e-mail address		
OTP Mobile Number		
Bank Linked		
Account No		

UPI	SELF	SPOUSE
Service Provider 2 Name: e.g GPay, Phone Pe, Amazon Pay, Mobikwick		
UPI ID / Virtual Payment Address (VPA)		
Username		
Password		
Security Question		
OTP e-mail address		
OTP Mobile Number		
Bank Linked		
Account No		

UPI	SELF	SPOUSE
Service Provider 3 Name: e.g GPay, Phone Pe, Amazon Pay, Mobikwick		
UPI ID / Virtual Payment Address (VPA)		
Username/ID		
Password		
Security Question		
OTP e-mail address		
OTP Mobile Number		
Bank Linked		
Account No		

UPI	CHILD 1	CHILD 2	CHILD 3
Service Provider 1 Name: e.g GPay, Phone Pe, Amazon Pay, Mobikwick			
UPI ID / Virtual Payment Address (VPA)			
Username/ID			
Password			
Security Question			
OTP e-mail address			
OTP Mobile Number			
Bank Linked			
Account No			

UPI	CHILD 1	CHILD 2	CHILD 3
Service Provider 2 Name: e.g GPay, Phone Pe, Amazon Pay, Mobikwick			
UPI ID / Virtual Payment Address (VPA)			
Username/ID			
Password			
Security Question			
OTP e-mail address			
OTP Mobile Number			
Bank Linked			
Account No			

UPI	CHILD 1	CHILD 2	CHILD 3
Service Provider 3 Name: e.g GPay, Phone Pe, Amazon Pay, Mobikwick			
UPI ID / Virtual Payment Address (VPA)			
Username/ID			
Password			
Security Question			
OTP e-mail address			
OTP Mobile Number			
Bank Linked			
Account No			

UPI	FATHER	MOTHER
Service Provider 1 Name: e.g GPay, Phone Pe, Amazon Pay, Mobikwick		
UPI ID / Virtual Payment Address (VPA)		
Username/ID		
Password		
Security Question		
OTP e-mail address		
OTP Mobile Number		
Bank Linked		
Account No		

UPI	FATHER	MOTHER
Service Provider 2 Name: e.g Gapy, Phone Pe, Amazon Pay, Mobikwick		
UPI ID / Virtual Payment Address (VPA)		
Username/ID		
Password		
Security Question		
OTP e-mail address		
OTP Mobile Number		
Bank Linked		
Account No		

UPI	FATHER	MOTHER
Service Provider 3 Name: e.g Gapy, Phone Pe, Amazon Pay, Mobikwick		
UPI ID / Virtual Payment Address (VPA)		
Username/ID		
Password		
Security Question		
OTP e-mail address		
OTP Mobile Number		
Bank Linked		
Account No		

2. PERSONAL BANK ACCOUNT

SELF	ACCOUNT 1	ACCOUNT 2	ACCOUNT 3
Bank Name			
Branch/IFSC Code			
RM - Name			
RM - Contact Number			
A/c Number			
A/c Type			
A/c Holder(s)			
Primary Account Holder			
Secondary Account Holder			

SELF	ACCOUNT 1	ACCOUNT 2	ACCOUNT 3
Mode of Operation			
Customer ID			
Nominee			
E-mail address for OTP			
Mobile Number for OTP			
Debit Card Number			
Debit Card Expiry			
Tap & Pay (Yes/No)			
Username/ID			
Password			

SPOUCE	ACCOUNT 1	ACCOUNT 2	ACCOUNT 3
Bank Name			
Branch/IFSC Code			
RM - Name			
RM - Contact Number			
A/c Number			
A/c Type			
A/c Holder(s)			
Primary Account Holder			
Secondary Account Holder			
Mode of Operation			

SPOUCE	ACCOUNT 1	ACCOUNT 2	ACCOUNT 3
Customer ID			
Nominee			
E-mail address for OTP			
Mobile Number for OTP			
Debit Card Number			
Debit Card Expiry			
Tap & Pay (Yes/No)			
Username/ID			
Password			

BANK A/C	CHILD 1	CHILD 2	CHILD 3
Bank Name			
Branch/IFSC Code			
RM - Name			
RM - Contact Number			
A/c Number			
A/c Type			
A/c Holder(s)			
Primary Account Holder			
Secondary Account Holder			
Mode of Operation			

BANK A/C	CHILD 1	CHILD 2	CHILD 3
Customer ID			
Nominee			
E-mail address for OTP			
Mobile Number for OTP			
Debit Card Number			
Debit Card Expiry			
Tap & Pay (Yes/No)			
Username/ ID			
Password			

FATHER	ACCOUNT 1	ACCOUNT 2	ACCOUNT 3
Bank Name			
Branch/IFSC Code			
RM - Name			
RM - Contact Number			
A/c Number			
A/c Type			
A/c Holder(s)			
Primary Account Holder			
Secondary Account Holder			
Mode of Operation			

FATHER	ACCOUNT 1	ACCOUNT 2	ACCOUNT 3
Customer ID			
Nominee			
E-mail address for OTP			
Mobile Number for OTP			
Debit Card Number			
Debit Card Expiry			
Tap & Pay (Yes/No)			
Username/ID			
Password			

MOTHER	ACCOUNT 1	ACCOUNT 2	ACCOUNT 3
Bank Name			
Branch/IFSC Code			
RM - Name			
RM - Contact Number			
A/c Number			
A/c Type			
A/c Holder(s)			
Primary Account Holder			
Secondary Account Holder			
Mode of Operation			

MOTHER	ACCOUNT 1	ACCOUNT 2	ACCOUNT 3
Customer ID			
Nominee			
E-mail address for OTP			
Mobile Number for OTP			
Debit Card Number			
Debit Card Expiry			
Tap & Pay (Yes/ No)			
Username/ID			
Password			

1. BUSINESS BANK ACCOUNT

	ACCOUNT 1	ACCOUNT 2
Bank Name		
Branch/IFSC Code		
A/c Number		
A/c Type		
A/c Holder(s)		
RM - Name		
RM - Contact Details		
Customer ID		
Nominee		
E-mail address for OTP		
Mobile Number for OTP		
Debit Card Number		
Debit Card Expiry Date		
Name on the Debit Card		
Primary Account Holder		
Secondary Account Holder		
Mode of Operation		
Debit Card Expiry		
Tap & Pay (Yes/No)		
Username/ID		
Password		

2. LOCKER DETAILS

SELF	LOCKER 1	LOCKER 2
Bank Name		
Branch/IFSC Code		
Locker No.		
Key No.		
A/c Holder(s)		
Primary Account Holder		
Secondary Account Holder		
RM - Name		
RM - Contact Details		
Mode of Operation		
Rent Renewal Date		
Nominee		
Operating Instructions		
Contents (*)		

SPOUSE	LOCKER 1	LOCKER 2
Bank Name		
Branch/IFSC Code		
Locker No.		
Key No.		
A/c Holder(s)		
Primary Account Holder		
Secondary Account Holder		
RM - Name		
RM - Contact Details		
Mode of Operation		
Rent Renewal Date		
Nominee		
Operating Instructions		
Contents (*)		

FATHER	LOCKER 1	LOCKER 2
Bank Name		
Branch/IFSC Code		
Locker No.		
Key No.		
A/c Holder(s)		
Primary Account Holder		
Secondary Account Holder		
RM - Name		
RM - Contact Details		
Mode of Operation		
Rent Renewal Date		
Nominee		
Operating Instructions		
Contents (*)		

MOTHER	LOCKER 1	LOCKER 2
Bank Name		
Branch/IFSC Code		
Locker No.		
Key No.		
A/c Holder(s)		
Primary Account Holder		
Secondary Account Holder		
RM - Name		
RM - Contact Details		
Mode of Operation		
Rent Renewal Date		
Nominee		
Operating Instructions		
Contents (*)		

3. PUBLIC PROVIDENT FUND (PPF)

PPF	SELF	SPOUSE
Bank Name		
Branch/IFSC Code		
RM - Name		
RM - Contact Details		
A/c No.		
A/c Opening Date		
15 years completion, date		
05 years extension completion date		
Loan against PPF, if any		
Withdrawal after 7 years lock-in, if any		
Nominee		
Remarks		

PPF	CHILD 1	CHILD 2	CHILD 3
Bank Name			
Branch/IFSC Code			
RM - Name			
RM - Contact Details			
A/c No.			
A/c Opening Date			
15 years completion, date			
05 years extension completion date			
Loan against PPF, if any			
Withdrawal after 7 years lock-in, if any			
Nominee			
Remarks			

PPF	FATHER	MOTHER
Bank Name		
Branch/IFSC Code		
RM - Name		
RM - Contact Details		
A/c No.		
A/c Opening Date		
15 years completion, date		
05 years extension completion date		
Loan against PPF, if any		
Withdrawal after 7 years lock-in, if any		
Nominee		
Remarks		

4. EMPLOYEE PROVIDENT FUND (EPF)/GRATUITY

EPF	SELF	SPOUSE
Bank Name		
Branch/IFSC Code		
RM - Name		
RM - Contact Details		
A/c No./UAN		
Nominee		
Organisation HR Personnel Name		
Organisation HR Personnel Contact Details		
Remarks		

EPF	FATHER	MOTHER
Bank Name		
Branch/IFSC Code		
RM - Name		
RM - Contact Details		
A/c No./UAN		
Nominee		
Organisation HR Personnel Name		
Organisation HR Personnel Contact Details		
Remarks		

5. NATIONAL PENSION SCHEME (NPS)

NPS	SELF	SPOUSE
PRAN		
Nominee		
Name of the Intermediary		
NPS Transfer from Pvt To Govt Date, if any		
NPS Transfer of Subscriber Acknowledgement No, if any		
Username/ID		
Password		
Secret Question		
Answer		

NPS	CHILD 1	CHILD 2	CHILD 3
PRAN			
Nominee			
Name of the Intermediary			
NPS Transfer from Pvt To Govt Date, if any			
NPS Transfer of Subscriber Acknowledgement No, if any			
Username/ID			
Password			
Secret Question			
Answer			

NPS	FATHER	MOTHER
PRAN		
Nominee		
Name of the Intermediary		
NPS Transfer from Pvt To Govt Date, if any		
NPS Transfer of Subscriber Acknowledgement No, if any		
Username/ID		
Password		
Secret Question		
Answer		

6. LIFE INSURANCE

Group Life Insurance from Employer

	INSURANCE COMPANY	POLICY NO	AMOUNT	CONTACT NO
Self				
Spouse				
Child 1				
Child 2				
Father				
Mother				
Father-in-law				
Mother-in-law				

Self-Purchase Policy

SELF	POLICY 1	POLICY 2	POLICY 3
Company			
RM - Name			
RM - Contact Details			
Policy Type			
Policy Number			
Sum Insured			
Premium Amount			
Premium Date			
Maturity Amount			
Empaneled Hospital Link			
TPA/Customer Service No.			
Address			
Nominee			
Username/ID			
Password			
Habits Declared in Previous Policy *			
Pre-Existing illness			

SPOUSE	POLICY 1	POLICY 2	POLICY 3
Company			
RM - Name			
RM - Contact Details			
Policy Type			
Policy Number			
Sum Insured			
Premium Amount			
Premium Date			
Maturity Amount			
Empaneled Hospital Link			
TPA/Customer Service No.			
Address			
Nominee			
Username/ID			
Password			
Habits Declared in Previous Policy *			
Pre-existing illness			

CHILD 1	POLICY 1	POLICY 2	POLICY 3
Company			
RM - Name			
RM - Contact Details			
Policy Type			
Policy Number			
Sum Insured			
Premium Amount			
Premium Date			
Maturity Amount			
Empaneled Hospital Link			
TPA/Customer Service No.			
Address			
Nominee			
Username/ID			
Password			
Habits Declared in Previous Policy *			
Pre-Existing illness			

CHILD 2	POLICY 1	POLICY 2	POLICY 3
Company			
RM - Name			
RM - Contact Details			
Policy Type			
Policy Number			
Sum Insured			
Premium Amount			
Premium Date			
Maturity Amount			
Empaneled Hospital Link			
TPA/Customer Service No.			
Address			
Nominee			
Username/ID			
Password			
Habits Declared in Previous Policy *			
Pre-existing illness			

CHILD 3	POLICY 1	POLICY 2	POLICY 3
Company			
RM - Name			
RM - Contact Details			
Policy Type			
Policy Number			
Sum Insured			
Premium Amount			
Premium Date			
Maturity Amount			
Empaneled Hospital Link			
TPA/Customer Service No.			
Address			
Nominee			
Username/ID			
Password			
Habits Declared in Previous Policy *			
Pre-existing illness			

FATHER	POLICY 1	POLICY 2	POLICY 3
Company			
RM - Name			
RM - Contact Details			
Policy Type			
Policy Number			
Sum Insured			
Premium Amount			
Premium Date			
Maturity Amount			
Empaneled Hospital Link			
TPA/Customer Service No.			
Address			
Nominee			
Username/ID			
Password			
Habits Declared in Previous Policy *			
Pre-existing illness			

MOTHER	POLICY 1	POLICY 2	POLICY 3
Company			
RM - Name			
RM - Contact Details			
Policy Type			
Policy Number			
Sum Insured			
Premium Amount			
Premium Date			
Maturity Amount			
Empaneled Hospital Link			
TPA/Customer Service No.			
Address			
Nominee			
Username/ID			
Password			
Habits Declared in Previous Policy *			
Pre-existing illness			

1. HEALTH INSURANCE

Group Health Insurance by Employer

	INSURANCE COMPANY	POLICY NO	AMOUNT	TPA CONTACT NO
Self				
Spouse				
Child 1				
Child 2				
Father				
Mother				
Father-in-law				
Mother-in-law				

Self-Purchased Policy

SELF	POLICY 1	POLICY 2
Company		
RM - Name		
RM - Contact Details		
Policy Type		
Policy Number		
Sum Insured		
Premium Amount		
Renewal Date		
Maturity Amount		
Empaneled Hospital Link		
TPA/Customer Service No.		
Address		
Nominee		
Username/ID		
Password		
Habits Declared in Previous Policy *		

SPOUSE	POLICY 1	POLICY 2
Company		
RM - Name		
RM - Contact Details		
Policy Type		
Policy Number		
Sum Insured		
Premium Amount		
Renewal Date		
Maturity Amount		
Empaneled Hospital Link		
TPA/Customer Service No.		
Address		
Nominee		
Username/ID		
Password		
Habits Declared in Previous Policy *		

CHILD 1	POLICY 1	POLICY 2
Company		
RM - Name		
RM - Contact Details		
Policy Type		
Policy Number		
Sum Insured		
Premium Amount		
Renewal Date		
Maturity Amount		
Empaneled Hospital Link		
TPA/Customer Service No.		
Address		
Nominee		
Username/ID		
Password		
Habits Declared in Previous Policy *		

CHILD 2	POLICY 1	POLICY 2
Company		
RM - Name		
RM - Contact Details		
Policy Type		
Policy Number		
Sum Insured		
Premium Amount		
Renewal Date		
Maturity Amount		
Empaneled Hospital Link		
TPA/Customer Service No.		
Address		
Nominee		
Username/ID		
Password		
Habits Declared in Previous Policy *		

CHILD 3	POLICY 1	POLICY 2
Company		
RM - Name		
RM - Contact Details		
Policy Type		
Policy Number		
Sum Insured		
Premium Amount		
Renewal Date		
Maturity Amount		
Empaneled Hospital Link		
TPA/Customer Service No.		
Address		
Nominee		
Username/ID		
Password		
Habits Declared in Previous Policy *		

2. GENERAL INSURANCE - MOTOR/HOME/OTHER

	POLICY 1	POLICY 2
Company		
Policy Type		
RM - Name		
RM - Contact Details		
Policy Number		
Sum Insured		
Premium Amount		
Renewal Date		
Maturity Amount		
Nominee		
Username/ID		
Password		
Deceleration made in policy		

	POLICY 1	POLICY 2
Company		
Policy Type		
RM - Name		
RM - Contact Details		
Policy Number		
Sum Insured		
Premium Amount		
Renewal Date		
Maturity Amount		
Nominee		
Username/ID		
Password		
Deceleration made in policy		

3. UNIT LINKED INSURANCE PLANS (ULIPs)

SELF	ULIP 1	ULIP 2
Plan Type		
Bank Name		
Branch/IFCS Code		
RM - Name		
RM - Contact Details		
Folio No.		
Sum Insured		
Maturity Amount		
Premium Payment term		
Premium Amount		
Premium Payment Frequency		
Nominee		
Username/ID		
Password		
Habits Declared in Previous Policy*		

SPOUSE	ULIP 1	ULIP 2
Plan Type		
Bank Name		
Branch/IFCS Code		
RM - Name		
RM - Contact Details		
Folio No.		
Sum Insured		
Maturity Amount		
Premium Payment term		
Premium Amount		
Premium Payment Frequency		
Nominee		
Username/ID		
Password		
Habits Declared in Previous Policy*		

CHILD 1	ULIP 1	ULIP 2
Plan Type		
Bank Name		
Branch/IFCS Code		
RM - Name		
RM - Contact Details		
Folio No.		
Sum Insured		
Maturity Amount		
Premium Payment term		
Premium Amount		
Premium Payment Frequency		
Nominee		
Username/ID		
Password		
Habits Declared in Previous Policy*		

CHILD 2	ULIP 1	ULIP 2
Plan Type		
Bank Name		
Branch/IFCS Code		
RM - Name		
RM - Contact Details		
Folio No.		
Sum Insured		
Maturity Amount		
Premium Payment term		
Premium Amount		
Premium Payment Frequency		
Nominee		
Username/ID		
Password		
Habits Declared in Previous Policy*		

CHILD 3	ULIP 1	ULIP 2
Plan Type		
Bank Name		
Branch/IFCS Code		
RM - Name		
RM - Contact Details		
Folio No.		
Sum Insured		
Maturity Amount		
Premium Payment term		
Premium Amount		
Premium Payment Frequency		
Nominee		
Username/ID		
Password		
Habits Declared in Previous Policy*		

FATHER	ULIP 1	ULIP 2
Plan Type		
Bank Name		
Branch/IFCS Code		
RM - Name		
RM - Contact Details		
Folio No.		
Sum Insured		
Maturity Amount		
Premium Payment term		
Premium Amount		
Premium Payment Frequency		
Nominee		
Username/ID		
Password		
Habits Declared in Previous Policy*		

MOTHER	ULIP 1	ULIP 2
Plan Type		
Bank Name		
Branch/IFCS Code		
RM - Name		
RM - Contact Details		
Folio No.		
Sum Insured		
Maturity Amount		
Premium Payment term		
Premium Amount		
Premium Payment Frequency		
Nominee		
Username/ID		
Password		
Habits Declared in Previous Policy*		

1. FIXED DEPOSITS (FDs)*

SELF	FD 1	FD 2	FD3
Bank Name			
Branch/IFCS Code			
Account No.			
RM - Name			
RM - Contact Details			
Linked Account No.			
Amount			
Maturity Date			
Maturity Amount			
Nominee			
Customer ID			
Username/ID			
Password			

SPOUSE	FD 1	FD 2	FD3
Bank Name			
Branch/IFCS Code			
Account No.			
RM - Name			
RM - Contact Details			
Linked Account No.			
Amount			
Maturity Date			
Maturity Amount			
Nominee			
Customer ID			
Username/ID			
Password			

CHILD 1	FD 1	FD 2	FD3
Bank Name			
Branch/IFCS Code			
Account No.			
RM - Name			
RM - Contact Details			
Linked Account No.			
Amount			
Maturity Date			
Maturity Amount			
Nominee			
Customer ID			
Username/ID			
Password			

CHILD 2	FD 1	FD 2	FD3
Bank Name			
Branch/IFCS Code			
Account No.			
RM - Name			
RM - Contact Details			
Linked Account No.			
Amount			
Maturity Date			
Maturity Amount			
Nominee			
Customer ID			
Username/ID			
Password			
CHILD 3	**FD 1**	**FD 2**	**FD3**

CHILD 2	FD 1	FD 2	FD3
Bank Name			
Branch/IFCS Code			
Account No.			
RM - Name			
RM - Contact Details			
Linked Account No.			
Amount			
Maturity Date			
Maturity Amount			
Nominee			
Customer ID			
Username/ID			
Password			

FATHER	FD 1	FD 2	FD3
Bank Name			
Branch/IFCS Code			
Account No.			
RM - Name			
RM - Contact Details			
Linked Account No.			
Amount			
Maturity Date			
Maturity Amount			
Nominee			
Customer ID			
Username/ID			
Password			
MOTHER	**FD 1**	**FD 2**	**FD3**

FATHER	FD 1	FD 2	FD3
Bank Name			
Branch/IFCS Code			
Account No.			
RM - Name			
RM - Contact Details			
Linked Account No.			
Amount			
Maturity Date			
Maturity Amount			
Nominee			
Customer ID			
Username/ID			
Password			

2. RECURRING DEPOSITS*

	RD 1	RD 2
Bank Name		
Branch/IFCS Code		
Account No.		
RM - Name		
RM - Contact Details		
Linked Account No.		
Monthly Amount		
Maturity Date		
Maturity Amount		
Nominee		
Username/ID		
Password		

3. DEMAT / TRADING ACCOUNT

SELF	ACCOUNT 1	ACCOUNT 2
Broker Name		
Demat A/c No.		
Trading A/c No.		
DP ID		
Client ID		
RM - Name		
RM - Contact Details		
Bank Name		
Linked Bank A/c No.		
Primary Account Holder		
Secondary Account Holder		
Mode of Operation		
OTP e-mail address		
OTP Mobile Number		
Estimated Portfolio Value		
Nominee		
Username/ID		
Password		

SPOUSE	ACCOUNT 1	ACCOUNT 2
Broker Name		
Demat A/c No.		
Trading A/c No.		
DP ID		
Client ID		
RM - Name		
RM - Contact Details		
Bank Name		
Linked Bank A/c No.		
Primary Account Holder		
Secondary Account Holder		
Mode of Operation		
OTP e-mail address		
OTP Mobile Number		
Estimated Portfolio Value		
Nominee		
Username/ID		
Password		

	CHILD 1	CHILD 2	CHILD 3
Broker Name			
Demat A/c No.			
Trading A/c No.			
DP ID			
Client ID			
RM - Name			
RM - Contact Details			
Bank Name			
Linked Bank A/c No.			
Primary Account Holder			
Secondary Account Holder			
Mode of Operation			
OTP e-mail address			
OTP Mobile Number			
Estimated Portfolio Value			
Nominee			
Username/ID			
Password			

FATHER	ACCOUNT 1	ACCOUNT 2
Broker Name		
Demat A/c No.		
Trading A/c No.		
DP ID		
Client ID		
RM - Name		
RM - Contact Details		
Bank Name		
Linked Bank A/c No.		
Primary Account Holder		
Secondary Account Holder		
Mode of Operation		
OTP e-mail address		
OTP Mobile Number		
Estimated Portfolio Value		
Nominee		
Username/ID		
Password		

MOTHER	ACCOUNT 1	ACCOUNT 2
Broker Name		
Demat A/c No.		
Trading A/c No.		
DP ID		
Client ID		
RM - Name		
RM - Contact Details		
Bank Name		
Linked Bank A/c No.		
Primary Account Holder		
Secondary Account Holder		
Mode of Operation		
OTP e-mail address		
OTP Mobile Number		
Estimated Portfolio Value		
Nominee		
Username/ID		
Password		

4. MUTUAL FUNDS*

SELF	MF 1	MF 2	MF3
Joint Holder 1			
Joint Holder 2			
Fund Name			
AMC Name			
Type			
Folio No.			
Amount			
Start Date			
End Date			
Linked Bank A/c No.			
SIP Date & Frequency			
Nominee			
Username/ID			
Password			

SPOUSE	MF 1	MF 2	MF3
Joint Holder 1			
Joint Holder 2			
Fund Name			
AMC Name			
Type			
Folio No.			
Amount			
Start Date			
End Date			
Linked Bank A/c No.			
SIP Date & Frequency			
Nominee			
Username/ID			
Password			

CHILD 1	MF 1	MF 2	MF3
Joint Holder 1			
Joint Holder 2			
Fund Name			
AMC Name			
Type			
Folio No.			
Amount			
Start Date			
End Date			
Linked Bank A/c No.			
SIP Date & Frequency			
Nominee			
Username/ID			
Password			

CHILD 2	MF 1	MF 2	MF3
Joint Holder 1			
Joint Holder 2			
Fund Name			
AMC Name			
Type			
Folio No.			
Amount			
Start Date			
End Date			
Linked Bank A/c No.			
SIP Date & Frequency			
Nominee			
Username/ID			
Password			

CHILD 3	MF 1	MF 2	MF3
Joint Holder 1			
Joint Holder 2			
Fund Name			
AMC Name			
Type			
Folio No.			
Amount			
Start Date			
End Date			
Linked Bank A/c No.			
SIP Date & Frequency			
Nominee			
Username/ID			
Password			

FATHER	MF 1	MF 2	MF3
Joint Holder 1			
Joint Holder 2			
Fund Name			
AMC Name			
Type			
Folio No.			
Amount			
Start Date			
End Date			
Linked Bank A/c No.			
SIP Date & Frequency			
Nominee			
Username/ID			
Password			

MOTHER	MF 1	MF 2	MF3
Joint Holder 1			
Joint Holder 2			
Fund Name			
AMC Name			
Type			
Folio No.			
Amount			
Start Date			
End Date			
Linked Bank A/c No.			
SIP Date & Frequency			
Nominee			
Username/ID			
Password			

5. CAMS KARVY DETAILS

Self	
Username/ID	
Password	
E-mail address for OTP	
Mobile Number for OTP	
Security Question/Code	

Spouse	
Username/ID	
Password	
E-mail address for OTP	
Mobile Number for OTP	
Security Question/Code	

Father	
Username/ID	
Password	
E-mail address for OTP	
Mobile Number for OTP	
Security Question/Code	

Mother	
Username/ID	
Password	
E-mail address for OTP	
Mobile Number for OTP	
Security Question/Code	

1. CREDIT CARDS

SELF	CARD 1	CARD 2	CARD 3
Issuer			
Card No.			
Type of Card Primary/Add-on			
Insurance Amount, if any			
Tap & Pay (Yes/ No) & Limit			
Nominee			
Username/ID			
Password			

SPOUSE	CARD 1	CARD 2	CARD 3
Issuer			
Card No.			
Type of Card Primary/Add-on			
Insurance Amount if any			
Tap & Pay (Yes/ No) & Limit			
Nominee			
Username/ID			
Password			

FATHER	CARD 1	CARD 2	CARD 3
Issuer			
Card No.			
Type of Card Primary/Add-on			
Insurance Amount if any			
Tap & Pay (Yes/ No) & Limit			
Nominee			
Username/ID			
Password			

MOTHER	CARD 1	CARD 2	CARD 3
Issuer			
Card No.			
Type of Card Primary/Add-on			
Insurance Amount if any			

MOTHER	CARD 1	CARD 2	CARD 3
Tap & Pay (Yes/No) & Limit			
Nominee			
Username/ID			
Password			

2. LOANS

SELF	LOAN 1	LOAN 2
Type		
Bank Name		
A/c No.		
Linked bank A/c No.		
Monthly EMI		
Last EMI Date		
Username/ID		
Password		

SPOUSE	LOAN 1	LOAN 2
Type		
Bank Name		
A/c No.		
Linked bank A/c No.		
Monthly EMI		
Last EMI Date		
Username/ID		
Password		

FATHER	LOAN 1	LOAN 2
Type		
Bank Name		
A/c No.		
Linked bank A/c No.		
Monthly EMI		
Last EMI Date		
Username/ID		
Password		

MOTHER	LOAN 1	LOAN 2
Type		
Bank Name		
A/c No.		
Linked bank A/c No.		
Monthly EMI		
Last EMI Date		
Username/ID		
Password		

3. BONDS

SELF	BOND 1	BOND 2	BOND 3
Bond Type			
Linked Bank A/c No.			
Bank Name			
Branch			
Folio No.			

SELF	BOND 1	BOND 2	BOND 3
Name of the Company			
No. of Bonds			
Lock-in Period			
Sum Invested			
Date of Purchase			
Maturity Amount			
Maturity Date			
Nominee			
Name of the RTA			
Image of the document in required			
Username/ID			
Password			

SPOUSE	BOND 1	BOND 2	BOND 3
Bond Type			
Linked Bank A/c No.			
Bank Name			
Branch			
Folio No.			
Name of the Company			
No. of Bonds			
Lock-in Period			
Sum Invested			
Date of Purchase			
Maturity Amount			
Maturity Date			
Nominee			
Name of the RTA			
Image of the document in required			
Username/ID			
Password			

FATHER	BOND 1	BOND 2	BOND 3
Bond Type			
Linked Bank A/c No.			
Bank Name			
Branch			
Folio No.			
Name of the Company			
No. of Bonds			
Lock-in Period			
Sum Invested			
Date of Purchase			
Maturity Amount			
Maturity Date			
Nominee			
Name of the RTA			
Image of the document in required			
Username/ID			
Password			

MOTHER	BOND 1	BOND 2	BOND 3
Bond Type			
Linked Bank A/c No.			
Bank Name			
Branch			
Folio No.			
Name of the Company			
No. of Bonds			
Lock-in Period			
Sum Invested			
Date of Purchase			
Maturity Amount			
Maturity Date			
Nominee			
Name of the RTA			
Image of the document in required			
Username/ID			
Password			

4. IMMOVABLE ASSETS / PROPERTY DETAILS*

Address of the Property 1	
Name of the Primary Owner	
Name of Joint Owner 1	
Name of Joint Owner 2	
Share Certificate No	
Distinctive No from:	
Distinctive No To:	
Society Manager Name	
Society Manager Mobile No	
Society Manager email	
Nomination and date of registration	
Details of Mortgage, if any	
Property Tax Details	

Address of the Property 2	
Name of the Primary Owner	
Name of Joint Owner 1	
Name of Joint Owner 2	
Share Certificate No	
Distinctive No from:	
Distinctive No To:	
Society Manager Name	
Society Manager Mobile No	
Society Manager email	
Nomination and date of registration	
Details of Mortgage, if any	
Property Tax Details	

Address of the Property 2	
Name of the Primary Owner	
Name of Joint Owner 1	
Name of Joint Owner 2	
Share Certificate No	
Distinctive No from:	
Distinctive No To:	
Society Manager Name	
Society Manager Mobile No	
Society Manager email	
Nomination and date of registration	
Details of Mortgage, if any	
Property Tax Details	

Address of the Property 3	
Name of the Primary Owner	
Name of Joint Owner 1	
Name of Joint Owner 2	
Share Certificate No	
Distinctive No from:	
Distinctive No To:	
Society Manager Name	
Society Manager Mobile No	
Society Manager email	
Nomination and date of registration	
Details of Mortgage, if any	
Property Tax Details	

Remarks:

5. **LEAVE AND LICENCE DETAILS:** If property given on leave and licence, then following details of the Tenant:

Details of the Property 1	
Address	
Name of the Tenant	
PAN NO of the Tenant	
Aadhar No of the Tenant	
Mobile No	
E-mail address	
Permanent Address	
Rent per month.	
Date of expiry of leave and licence	

Details of the Property 2	
Address	
Name of the Tenant	
PAN NO of the Tenant	
Aadhar No of the Tenant	
Mobile No	
E-mail address	
Permanent Address	
Rent per month.	
Date of expiry of leave and licence	

Details of the Property 3	
Address	
Name of the Tenant	
PAN NO of the Tenant	
Aadhar No of the Tenant	
Mobile No	
E-mail address	
Permanent Address	
Rent per month.	
Date of expiry of leave and licence	

1. Jewellery Details:

Jewellery Type	Last appraised value	Description (Brand name, carat, colour, clarity, etc.)	Date of Ownership	Identification No	Photograph*

*Be sure to photograph each piece two ways: one, up close to show details and two, with your face in the photo to prove that you are the owner of the piece.

2. Digilocker

https://www.digilocker.gov.in/

DIGILOCKER DETAILS	AADHAR NO	SIX DIGIT PIN
Self		
Spouse		
Child 1		
Child 2		
Child 3		
Father		
Mother		

3. Government Scheme Details

Name of the Scheme	Holding Pattern	Account No	Remarks
Atal Pension Yogna (APY) SELF			
Atal Pension Yogna (APY) SPOUSE			
Atal Pension Yogna (APY) FATHER			
Atal Pension Yogna (APY) MOTHER			
Sukanya Samirdi Yogna CHILD 1			

Name of the Scheme	Holding Pattern	Account No	Remarks
Sukanya Samirdi Yogna CHILD 2			
Sukanya Samirdi Yogna CHILD 3			
Senior Citizens Savings Scheme (Father)			
Senior Citizens Savings Scheme (Mother)			
Pradhan Mantri Suraksha Bima Yojana (PMSBY) SELF			
Pradhan Mantri Suraksha Bima Yojana (PMSBY) SPOUSE			
Pradhan Mantri Suraksha Bima Yojana (PMSBY) FATHER			
Pradhan Mantri Suraksha Bima Yojana (PMSBY) MOTHER			
Pradhan Mantri Jeevan Jyoti Bima Yojana (PMJJBY) SELF			
Pradhan Mantri Jeevan Jyoti Bima Yojana (PMJJBY) SPOUSE			
Pradhan Mantri Jeevan Jyoti Bima Yojana (PMJJBY) FATHER			
Pradhan Mantri Jeevan Jyoti Bima Yojana (PMJJBY) MOTHER			

4. Ayushman Bharat Health Account Details

website: https://healthid.ndhm.gov.in/

ABHA DETAILS	ABHA ADDRESS	ABHA NUMBER	MOBILE NO	Registered e-mail address:
Self				
Spouse				
Child 1				
Child 2				
Child 3				
Father				
Mother				

5. Wills

Date of the Will	
Location of Original Will	
Name of the Executor	
Contact No:	
Address of the Executor	
Name of Witness 1	
Contact No	
Address	
Name of Witness 2	
Contact No	
Address	

Date of the Will	
Location of Copies of Will	
Change in Will Date & Reference to Notes Page	
Change in Will Date & Reference to Notes Page	
Change in Will Date & Reference to Notes Page	

6. LOCATION OF IMPORTANT DOCUMENTS

NAME OF THE DOCUMENT	LOCATION	REMARKS
Birth Certificate		
Death Certificate, If Any		
PAN Card		
AADHAR Card		
Voter ID Card		

NAME OF THE DOCUMENT	LOCATION	REMARKS
Passports		
Ration Card		
Chequebooks		
Driving Licence		
Vaccination Certificate		
Educational Certificates		
Marriage Certificate		
Loan Documents		
Tax Records		
Insurance Documents		
Mediclaim Documents		
Medical Records		
Vehicle Documents		
Power Of Attorney		

NAME OF THE DOCUMENT	LOCATION	REMARKS
Property Papers		
Leave and Licence Papers		
Locker Keys		
Other Important Keys		
Utility Bills		
Warranty Cards of Appliances & Assets		
Club Memberships		
Hospital Discharge Summary		
Habits as declared in Insurance		
Bill of Exchange		
Any Other Documents		

NAME OF THE DOCUMENT	LOCATION	REMARKS

7. MASTER WORD DOCUMENT OF PASSWORD:

Name of the Device:

Hint:

Location in the Device:

Password:

Hint:

8. INTERNATIONAL ASSETS DETAILS:

9. INTELLECTUAL PROPERTY AND OTHER ASSETS

10. MONEY OWED TO YOU.

NAME	MOBILE NO	DUE DATE	AMOUNT	LOCATION OF BILL OF EXCHANGE

You may wish to write the terms, conditions and interest rate in the Notes Section

11. MONEY OWED BY YOU.

NAME	MOBILE NO	DUE DATE	AMOUNT	LOCATION OF BILL OF EXCHANGE

You may wish to write the terms, conditions, and interest rate in the Notes Section

Chapter 10

Health is Wealth - The Importance of Financial Wellness

"Health is wealth" - It is a saying we all know well, but have you ever considered the importance of your financial health check-up?

This is the seventh story that made me think about the changes in my priorities as I grew older. As we transition from one phase of life to another, whether it's marriage, the birth of a child, buying a house, or nearing retirement, our financial needs and priorities change.

As I approach my 40th birthday on November 18, 2023, I had a thought-provoking conversation with my rakhi sister, Gayatri Tahiliani Shakrani, and her husband, Jitendra (Jeet), both skilled surgeons specialising in oncology and urology, respectively. We met for Raksha Bandhan, and they advised me, as I was turning 40, to undergo regular health check-ups, given that most of us have vitamin D deficiencies, and women often have haemoglobin concerns. It is advisable to have a complete body check-up, at least annually, we all agree.

This conversation made me reflect on the saying "health is wealth." Indeed, if you have all the money in the world but no health, what is the use of that wealth? I wanted to sensitise my readers to the fact that health is a crucial element. If you have good health, you can always generate more wealth, but if you don't have good health, it will drain most of your wealth.

However, what I want to stress is that financial health is as important as physical health. It is equally important to take care of one's financial wellness.

Financial Wellness and Its Importance

Financial wellness is a crucial aspect of our lives that encompasses the overall financial health of an individual, and it involves the process of learning how to successfully manage financial expenses. Financial wellness is about a person's control over his or her financial life, having an emergency savings fund, being able to meet financial goals, and securing our financial future.

Just like exercise and healthy eating are essential for preventive health care, reviewing your portfolio, developing a habit of savings and investments, ensuring that you pay your insurance premiums and credit card bills on time, and making finance a part of dinner table conversations are good habits for financial well-being.

As in healthcare, and in financial health, too, prevention is better than cure. The same principles apply to both healthcare and financial wellness.

Just like a regular health check-up can detect potential issues and lead to better health outcomes, a regular financial check-up can help ensure that you're on track to meet your financial goals and provide you peace of mind.

Just as one must undergo an annual health check-up, a financial health check-up is also essential. My wife and I meet our Chartered Accountant, CA Viral Mehta from Kiran Mehta and Company, every year for my annual wealth check-up. They are 5th generation Chartered Accountants and have become more like family.

Just as we need a doctor, we also need finance experts to advise us on important matters. We also visit our financial planner/wealth manager. It is vital to ask the right questions to the doctor. If we don't communicate our concerns accurately, the doctor won't be able to diagnose our illness. Similarly, we must ask the right questions and inform our CA about our concerns.

For example:

1. How can I save more tax?
2. What if I take a Home Loan? Will I be able to save tax?

3. Which tax regime is better, old or new?
4. Should I opt for presumptive taxation or maintain detailed books of accounts?
5. Can I gift money to my loved ones without gift tax?
6. How can I optimise my income tax deductions within my family?
7. I have bought a new car; can I claim depreciation?

Please don't get me wrong; I am a salaried person and an honest taxpayer. The objective is not to evade tax but to use the provisions within the law to save tax wherever possible.

So, your annual financial health check-up is as vital as your physical health check-up. Meet your CA to look at your taxation and your Financial Planner or Investment Adviser to understand your savings and investment portfolio. You may want to nurture the good schemes and assets and weed out the underperformers or the troublemakers in your financial portfolio.

I would also recommend that, just as you might seek a second opinion from another doctor, there is no harm in getting a second opinion from another expert.

Likewise, besides meeting our CA, we also consulted our Insurance Consultant, Ms. Kirti Motwani. She has known all four generations of our family, from my grandmother to my daughter. When we met with an accident in 2006, an emergency I have recounted in Chapter 2 as a Black Swan event, she was the one who helped us sail through the crisis, even though she was not our health insurance agent at the time. She stood by us in that challenging time and took it upon herself to write letters to the Insurance Company's Third-Party Administrator (TPA) and secure cashless facilities wherever possible. We were assured that she was there for us, no matter what. Kirti Aunty was rock-solid with us, and even today, she handles all our family's insurance needs. It was at this time that I realised, even though I had worked in the financial market, it was crucial to be with the right investment advisers, too.

Just like doctors, CAs, and Investment Advisers are like family. Be transparent, and share your concerns, and they will appreciate your honesty and rationale.

Your advisers, whether they are Chartered Accountants, Financial Planners, or Insurance Consultants, play a pivotal role in your financial well-being. It is essential to have advisers who not only have the expertise but also genuinely care for you and have your best interests at heart.

Also, remember that the most important financial discipline is to update your Wealth Diary regularly; your financial 'doctor' can know about your financial health only if you have all the reports ready.

So, dear readers, please remember to get your Financial Health Check-up done, at least once, annually.

Tips on Choosing the Right Financial Adviser:

Choosing the right financial adviser is crucial for your financial health and well-being. Here are some tips that can help you in selecting the right financial adviser:

1. **Understand Your Needs:** Before you start looking for a financial adviser, it is essential to understand your needs. Are you looking for help with investment management, retirement planning, tax planning, estate planning, or something else?
2. **Check Qualifications:** Make sure that the adviser has the necessary qualifications and certifications. Chartered Accountants (CAs) and SEBI registered Investment Advisers enjoy some of the most respected credentials in the Finance Industry.
3. **Experience Matters:** Look for an adviser with experience in the areas that matter most to you. For example, if you are near retirement, you might want an adviser who specialises in retirement planning.
4. **Fee Structure:** Understand how the adviser is compensated. Some advisers are fee-only, which means they only charge a fee for their services and do not receive any commissions. Others may charge a commission on the products they sell. It is essential to understand and be comfortable with the adviser's fee structure.
5. **Fiduciary Duty:** A fiduciary is an adviser who is legally obligated to act in your best interest. It is essential to know whether your adviser is a fiduciary or not.

6. **Communication Style:** Make sure that the adviser's communication style matches yours. Do you prefer to communicate via email, phone, or in-person meetings? Make sure your adviser is willing to communicate in the ways that work best for you.
7. **Check References:** Ask for references from current clients. It is always a good idea to speak to other clients to get a sense of what it is like to work with the adviser.
8. **Ask Questions:** Don't be afraid to ask questions. You should feel comfortable asking your adviser any questions that you have about your financial situation, their recommendations, or any other concerns that you may have.
9. **Genuinely Interested to Help You:** Look for an adviser who shows a genuine interest in helping you achieve your financial goals, rather than just focusing on commissions and fees. An adviser who takes the time to understand your unique needs and circumstances and provides personalised recommendations is more likely to have your best interests at heart.

Chapter 11

"Money: A Universal Language"

After reviewing all the outcomes of studies conducted on financial literacy, I was confronted with a revelation, an understanding of something so fundamental, yet so frequently overlooked. It was the realisation that irrespective of one's background, profession, or social standing, we are all inexorably linked by a shared relationship with money. It is the currency that weaves its way through our lives, dictating choices, influencing decisions, and setting the course for our future. Everyone, from the CEOs sitting in their plush offices to the security guards patrolling the premises, the polished politicians or the passionate professors, the dedicated doctors or the intellectual lawyers, even down to the diligent peons or the wise principals, all have to face up to the reality of financial decisions in their lives.

This understanding was accompanied by another - that financial literacy is not a luxury but a necessity. I realised the vital role of financial knowledge in empowering individuals, offering them a means of improving their lives, not only monetarily but also in terms of quality and freedom. And I realised my place in this scheme of things. The prospect of acquiring and disseminating this vital knowledge became my beacon, the lighthouse guiding my way amidst the turbulent seas of life.

Suddenly, the role of money in my life, and in the lives of others, took on an entirely new dimension. Money was no longer just a means to an end, but a tool, a language that needed to be mastered for optimal navigation of the world we live in. It was at this juncture that I accepted the responsibility of harnessing my financial knowledge, not just for my personal gain but as a service to others. My mission became clear; I was to equip as many people as possible with the understanding that could transform their financial lives. This was the juncture where my personal and professional trajectories aligned, morphing into a singular pathway that would guide the subsequent chapters of my life.

As we journey through life, making decisions that shape our futures, it becomes imperative that we understand the role of finances in this journey. Financial literacy is not just about knowing how to balance a chequebook or understanding the difference between stocks and bonds. It is a broader understanding of how to earn, manage, invest, and donate money responsibly. And it is something that everyone should strive to achieve.

In a world that is becoming increasingly complex, where our economic systems are interwoven with global events, and where our personal financial decisions can have profound effects on our lives, it is more important than ever to be financially literate. It empowers us to make informed decisions, protects us from fraud, and helps us achieve our personal and financial goals.

Yet, too many of us lack the fundamental knowledge required to make sound financial decisions. Whether it is a lack of access and education, or simply not knowing where to start, this gap in knowledge is causing real harm to individuals, families, and communities around the world.

Therefore, I appeal to each and every one of you to take this matter into your own hands. Start by educating yourself on the basics of personal finance. Understand your income, track your expenses, create a budget, start saving, and learn about investments. These are all crucial steps in becoming financially literate.

In our journey towards becoming financially literate, we might face several obstacles. When encountering these, remember a wise saying from my former boss, B. Gopkumar, who would ask, "Is it a skill issue or a will issue?" In the context of financial literacy, a 'skill issue' would mean a lack of knowledge or understanding about money matters. This can be overcome by education, self-learning, attending financial literacy programmes, or seeking advice from financial experts.

On the other hand, a 'will issue' might mean you are unmotivated or procrastinating on becoming financially literate. Remember, the road to financial well-being is not a passive one. It requires active engagement and continuous learning. It is not just about earning money but understanding how to manage, grow, and protect it. So, I urge everyone not to delay or underestimate the power of financial literacy. Start today because when it comes to personal finance, both skill and will matter.

Remember, financial literacy is not an end in itself but a means to an end - a secure, comfortable, and fulfilling life. It is never too late to start learning, and the benefits you'll reap are well worth the effort. In the age of information, there are numerous resources available to aid you on this journey.

Let us strive to be a financially literate society. Not only will this lead to improved individual financial well-being, but also a more stable and prosperous world. Let us make active efforts to understand our finances today so we can secure a better tomorrow for ourselves and our families.

The Wealth Diary: Your Personal Financial Record is more than just your income-expenditure ledger. It is an interactive and dynamic tool designed to encourage financial literacy, a lifelong learning experience in the realm of money and investment. By linking the conventional practice of record-keeping with the vast field of financial knowledge, this Diary promises a well-rounded and deeper comprehension of personal finance.

This Diary isn't simply about recording transactions; it is about exploring the broader context of one's financial landscape - tracking investments, gauging the implications of debts, and setting and monitoring financial goals. The "Wealth Diary" enables you to observe and make sense of your unique financial world. It unveils patterns, brings clarity to your spending habits, and enables strategic planning for future financial decisions.

Moreover, the Diary is designed to promote continuous learning. It is not merely a static repository of past financial actions but rather a progressive chronicle of your financial journey. It serves as a guide to understanding the ever-evolving complexities of personal finances and encourages responsible and informed decisions to secure a stable financial future. This, the "Wealth Diary," doesn't just record your present; it also helps to shape your future.

For me, it is my Wealth Diary. What would you like to call it?
Bon Voyage!!!

A United Appeal for Financial Literacy in India: Achieving Financial Independence

Financial independence is a crucial component of a nation's overall health and prosperity, and achieving it is not the sole responsibility of an individual or a single organisation. It is a shared responsibility that requires a collective effort from all stakeholders - the government, private sector, non-profit organisations, teachers, and citizens.

When people are financially literate and independent, they can make informed decisions about their money, leading to better financial outcomes for themselves and their families. This, in turn, contributes to a stronger and more resilient economy.

Therefore, it is in the best interests of all stakeholders to work together towards this common goal. By collaborating and supporting one another, we can create a stronger and more financially secure society, which benefits everyone.

In this 75th year of our independence, as we reflect on our journey as a nation and look towards the future, let us come together to build a financially literate and independent society. I appeal to all relevant stakeholders to contribute to this noble cause and help in the nation-building process. Together, we can create a legacy of financial literacy and independence that will be cherished by future generations.

Please find below the unified appeal to all stakeholders.

Dear Esteemed Stakeholders,

As I reflect on the significance and urgency of financial literacy, I am acutely aware that this mission – to make India financially literate – cannot be travelled alone. A nation of over 1.4 billion people requires the concerted effort of every individual and institution with the ability and will to contribute.

An Appeal to Educators:

Being an academic myself for more than 14 years, I have observed the power and moral responsibility that we, as educators, carry in shaping society. We face considerable academic and administrative pressures daily completing the curriculum, conducting assessments, striving for excellence, and fostering holistic student development. Amidst these demands, introducing a new initiative like financial literacy may seem daunting. But, as educators responsible for moulding future citizens, we bear a profound responsibility. Financial literacy is not merely a subject; it is a vital life skill, a cornerstone of personal empowerment and societal progress. I earnestly appeal to each of us to embrace financial literacy not as an additional burden but as a sacred mission. Let us equip our students with the tools they need to navigate the complex world of finance responsibly.

A Call to Government Bodies:

To enact systemic change, policies must evolve. Government bodies at various levels have the authority to institutionalise financial literacy as a core component of our education system. I urge you to recognise financial literacy as a national priority, drafting policies that make its education mandatory across schools and colleges in India.

A Request to Financial Institutions:

Financial institutions - including banks, investment companies, and insurance agencies — are central to this endeavour. I call upon you to leverage your resources and expertise, creating accessible, easy-to-understand resources and conducting workshops that can be introduced in academic institutions and local communities, as it is your fiduciary duty to provide a responsible financial ecosystem to all your customers.

To Non-Governmental Organisations (NGOs):
Your capacity to reach marginalised and underprivileged communities is unparalleled. I appeal to you to take financial literacy to the grassroots level, educating those who would otherwise remain untouched by these essential life skills.

A Plea to Parents and Guardians:
The home is the child's first school. Open dialogues about money, savings, and financial planning should be normalised in our families. I implore parents and guardians to engage in transparent discussions about finances with their children, setting the stage for a financially literate next generation.

Conclusion:
This is not just a mission; this is our shared mission as proud citizens of India. As our great nation celebrates 75 years of independence, it is a poignant moment to reflect on the essence of true freedom. Freedom is not merely political; it is also social and economic. True freedom is when each and every citizen, irrespective of their background, can navigate their lives with confidence, security, and dignity.

Our beloved India has come a long way in its journey as a sovereign nation. But to propel our country into a future where independence is meaningful and deeply rooted, we must strive for financial freedom for all. It is only when our people are financially literate that they can take control of their economic destiny, breaking the chains of debt, avoiding the pitfalls of financial fraud, and building a life of stability and prosperity.

Financial literacy is not just about understanding money; it is about empowering individuals to make informed decisions that affect their daily lives. It is the bridge that can lead to an equitable society, reducing the gaping disparities that still exist among different strata of our populace. It is the key to a prosperous India, where opportunities don't just belong to a select few, but are accessible to all.

As India steps into the next chapter of its journey post-75 years of independence, let us all—educators, government bodies, financial institutions, NGOs, and families alike—join hands to make financial literacy a fundamental right, not a privilege. This is the path to true empowerment, the road to a more equitable and prosperous India.

Let us together pledge that our mission for financial literacy will be the cornerstone of India's true freedom.

Thank you for considering this appeal. Together, we have the power to shape a brighter, more secure future for our nation.

With utmost respect,

Dr. Navin M. Punjabi

Author

The Wealth Diary

List of Essential Resources

To assist investors in navigating the vast landscape of the financial sector, we have curated a list of essential resources. These links not only encompass the securities market but also delve into banking, insurance, pensions, and taxation. Whether you are seeking information or need to raise concerns, this compilation ensures single-point access.

Investors are encouraged to utilise these resources to enrich their understanding, clarify doubts, and raise any concerns they might have. Ensuring transparency and ease of access, these links aim to promote an informed and proactive investor community.

Useful Websites, Mobile Applications, e-mails, and Toll-Free No on Investor Education and Awareness Initiatives

Name of the Institution	Website
Association of Mutual Funds in India (AMFI)	https://www.amfiindia.com/
Bima Bharosa - An Integrated Grievance Management Portal (Earlier Known as IGMS)	https://bimabharosa.irdai.gov.in/
Bombay Stock Exchange Ltd (BSE Ltd)	https://www.bseindia.com/
Bombay Stock Exchange Investor Protection Fund (BSE IPF)	https://www.bseipf.com/
Central Board of Indirect Taxes & Custom CBIC	https://www.cbic.gov.in/

Name of the Institution	Website
Central Depository Services (India) Limited (CDSL)	https://www.cdslindia.com/
Centralised Public Grievance Redress And Monitoring System (CPGRAM)	https://www.pgportal.gov.in/
Jagho Grihak Jago Consumer Support Portal	https://consumerhelpline.gov.in/index.php
Calcutta Stock Exchange (CSE)	https://www.cse-india.com/
Department of Consumers Affair (DCA)	https://consumeraffairs.nic.in/
Department Of Financial Services (DFS)	https://financialservices.gov.in/
Department of Telecommunication, Central Equipment Identity Register	https://www.ceir.gov.in/
Deposit Insurance and Credit Guarantee Corporation (DICGC)	https://www.dicgc.org.in/
Goods and Services Tax (GST)	https://www.gst.gov.in/
Institute of Chartered Accountants of India (ICIA)	https://www.icai.org/
The Institute of Cost Accountants of India (ICMAI)	https://icmai.in/icmai/
Institute of Company Secretaries of India (ICSI)	https://www.icsi.edu/home/
Investor Education and Protection Fund Authority (IEPFA)	https://www.iepf.gov.in
Investor Education and Welfare Association (IEWA)	http://iewa.in/
Indian Institute of Corporate Affairs (IICA)	https://iica.nic.in/
Income Tax Department	https://incometaxindia.gov.in
Insurance Information Bureau (IIB)	https://iib.gov.in/
Insurance Regulatory and Development Authority of India (IRDAI)	https://irdai.gov.in/
IRDA Consumer Education Website	www.policyholder.gov.in

Name of the Institution	Website
Krisha Foundation	www.krishafoundation.in
Ministry of Corporate Affairs	https://www.mca.gov.in
The Multi-Commodity Exchange of India Limited (MCX)	https://www.mcxindia.com/
Ministry Of Finance	https://www.finmin.nic.in/
Metropolitan Stock Exchange of India Limited (MSE)	https://www.msei.in/
National Bank for Agriculture and Rural Development (NABARD)	https://www.nabard.org/
National Commodity and Derivatives Exchange Limited (NCDEX)	https://www.ncdex.com
National Cyber Crime Reporting Portal	https://cybercrime.gov.in/
National Centre for Financial Education	https://www.ncfe.org.in/
National Foundation for Corporate Governance (NFCG)	https://www.nfcg.in/
National Financial Reporting Authority (NFRA)	https://nfra.gov.in/
National Institute of Securities Markets (NISM)	https://www.nism.ac.in/
National Payments Corporation of India (NPCI)	https://www.npci.org.in/
National Securities Depository Limited (NSDL)	https://www.nsdl.co.in
National Stock Exchange (NSE)	https://www.nseindia.com/
Nehru Yuva Kendra Sangathan	https://nyks.nic.in/
Pension Fund Regulatory and Development Authority (PFRDA)	https://www.pfrda.org.in/
Reserve Bank of India	https://rbi.org.in/
Reserve Bank of India, Financial Education	https://www.rbi.org.in/FinancialEducation/Home.aspx

Name of the Institution	Website
Reserve Bank of India Complaint Management System	https://cms.rbi.org.in/
Right to Information (RTI)	https://rtionline.gov.in/
Small Industries Development Bank of India	https://www.sidbi.in/en
Securities and Exchange Board of India (SEBI)	https://www.sebi.gov.in/
SEBI Investor Website	https://investor.sebi.gov.in/
SEBI Complaints REdress System (SCORES)	https://scores.gov.in
SMARTODR	https://smartodr.in/
Unclaimed Deposits Gateway To Access inforMation	https://udgam.rbi.org.in/
Watch Out Investors	https://www.watchoutinvestors.com

Mobile Phone Applications available on Android and Apple phones:

SAARTHI

SEBI COmplaints REdress System - SCORES

National Consumer Helpline – NCH

Investor Charter:

Investor Charter of SEBI: https://investor.sebi.gov.in/Investor-charter.html

Investor Charter - Stock Exchanges: https://investor.sebi.gov.in/Investor-charter-flagA.html

Investor Charter – Depositories: https://investor.sebi.gov.in/Investor-charter-flagB.html

One can go to the website of the concerned Mutual Fund and other Financial Institutions to read their respective Investor Charter.

Toll-free number of Financial Sector Regulators

Reserve Bank of India (RBI) - 14440

Fraudulent transaction in your bank account? Limit your loss. Notify your bank immediately. For more details, give a missed call on **14440**. toll-free number – **14448 (9:30 am to 5:15 pm)** – is also being operationalised in Hindi, English and eight regional languages, to begin with, and will be expanded to cover other Indian languages in due course. The Contact Centre will provide information/clarifications regarding the alternate grievance redress mechanism of RBI and guide complainants in filing a complaint.

Securities Exchange Boards of India (SEBI) - 1800 266 7575 or 1800 22 7575

To facilitate replies to various queries of the general public on matters relating to the securities market, SEBI has undertaken a new initiative and launched toll-free helpline service number **1800 266 7575 or 1800 22 7575**

Insurance Regulatory and Development Authority of India (IRDAI) -

IRDA Grievance Call Centre

Toll-Free Number: **155255 (or) 1800 4254 732**

Timings: **8 AM to 8 PM — (Monday to Saturday)**

Pension Fund Regulatory and Development Authority (PFRDA)

NPS Information desk: 1800 110 708

APY Information desk: 1800 110 069

National Stock Exchange (NSE)

Toll-Free Number: 1800 266 0050

Timings: 9:30 AM to 5:45 PM (Monday to Friday)

E-mail: ignse@nse.co.in

Address: National Stock Exchange of India Ltd, Exchange Plaza, C-1, Block G, Bandra Kurla Complex, Bandra (E), Mumbai – 400 051

Investor Education and Protection Fund Authority (IEPFA)

Ministry of Corporate Affairs, Government of India

Contact Details: 1800 114 667

E-mail: iepfgrievances[at]mca[dot]gov[dot]in

Address: Ground Floor, JeevanVihar Building, 3, Sansad Marg, New Delhi – 110001

National Cyber Crime Reporting Portal

Toll-Free No for Cyber Financial Fraud: 1930 (24*7)

Department of Telecommunication, Central Equipment Identity Register

Toll-Free No: **14422**

E-mail: ceir.support@cdot.in

Department of Consumer Affairs, Ministry of Consumer Affairs, Food & Public Distribution

National Consumer Helpline (NCH), Government of India

Toll-Free No: 1800-11-4000 or 1951

(All Days Except National Holidays (08:00 AM To 08:00 PM)

Whatsapp No: +91 8800001915

Know Your Mobile (KYM)

Through KYM, you can check the validity of your mobile device even before buying it. IMEI is written on the mobile packaging box. It could be found on the mobile bill/invoice. From your mobile you can check the IMEI number by dialling ***#06#,** IMEI number will be shown on mobile screen. If the status of the mobile is shown as black-listed, duplicate or already in use, please avoid buying the mobile. KYM could be used through any of the following three methods.

1. Type KYM <15 digit IMEI number> from your mobile and send the SMS to 14422.
2. Download the KYM app from Play Store (for Android) or from App Store (for iOS).
3. Verification on the website: https://www.ceir.gov.in/Device/CeirImeiVerification.jsp

Concerned National Strategies:
National Strategy for Financial Education –

https://www.rbi.org.in/Scripts/PublicationReportDetails.aspx?UrlPage=&ID=1156#ES

National Strategy for Financial Inclusion – https://www.rbi.org.in/Scripts/PublicationReportDetails.aspx?UrlPage=&ID=1154

While every effort has been made to make this resource comprehensive and forward-thinking, it must be remembered that personal finance is an evolving field. With changing times and technological advancements, new dimensions or avenues may arise that need to be addressed. These note pages are specifically designed for that purpose.

Whether it is a new type of investment, a novel financial tool that you have encountered, or any other relevant information not covered in the preceding sections, feel free to jot it down here. It is always good to have a space where you can capture evolving thoughts and financial directions that are part of your unique journey.

Additionally, if there are personal details, memories, or experiences associated with your financial milestones, these pages provide an ideal space to record them. After all, personal finance is as much about numbers as it is about the stories and experiences behind those numbers.

Notes

Notes

Notes

Notes

Notes

Notes

Notes

Notes

Notes

Your financial journey is personal and unique. While guidance can be provided, the path you carve out, based on your experiences and decisions, is yours alone. Use these pages to capture the essence of that journey, ensuring you have all the information you need at your fingertips.

Remember, the most successful financial plans are those that evolve and adapt to the ever-changing landscape of life and technology. Stay curious, stay informed, and most importantly, stay proactive.

I try and reduce myself to an almost blank slate and hope to God that I am creative.

- Ben Kingsley

www.ingramcontent.com/pod-product-compliance
Lightning Source LLC
LaVergne TN
LVHW100257210926
848480LV00003B/946